Dear Reader

The objective of Kendo World is to disseminate information that will help the international community of kendo aficionados in their study of the perennial path of traditional Japanese swordsmanship and related arts. Your purchase of this publication helps the Kendo World team travel around Japan to interview famous sensei, cover important kendo events, and pay translators for their tireless work deciphering kendo wisdom. We appreciate your continued support of Kendo World's aims to promote the beautiful art of kendo. If you are reading this publication on anything other than one of our authorised digital platforms (e.g. ZINIO, Kindle, iBooks), or in "Print on Demand" paper form via Amazon, then you are in possession of pirated material. As fellow kenshi, we appeal to your conscience in the hope that you refuse to participate in illegal file sharing of our copyrighted material. We agree that information belongs to everybody, but spare a thought for the time, effort, and resources that are required to bring it to you. Pirating is stealing. Without your backing, Kendo World will die. We don't want to die yet because there is still so much to do…

Happy reading and thank you.

Kendo World Team

Carbon Shinai
カーボンシナイ

CF-Type

DB-Type

K1-Type

K2-Type

Orange　Red　Yellow

We have improved the official Carbon Shinai rubber stopper.

The NEW official rubber stopper.

¥300 (domestic Japanese price)

WARNING!! Never use anything other than our official rubber stopper on your Carbon Shinai !!

When using your Carbon Shinai.....

1. To prevent injury, please use our official rubber stopper. Do not use stoppers made for conventional bamboo shinai on your Carbon Shinai, as there is a risk of injury to your opponent if the tip breaks through and enters their men grill.

2. When choosing a sakigawa (leather tip), make sure that it is more than 5cm in length and completely covers our rubber stopper. If the sakigawa is shorter than 5cm, there is a risk of injury to your opponent if a slat slips out and enters their men grill.

3. Do not shave the plastic surface of your Carbon Shinai. If you shave the surface, the black carbon fiber will be exposed, causing damage that may result in injury to your opponent.

4. Always check the condition of the surface of your Carbon Shinai before and during use. As soon as you notice any cracks, or peeling of the surface, or if black carbon fiber is exposed on any part of the outside, inside or edges of the Shinai, or you notice any other damage, stop using the shinai immediately. There is a danger of injury to your opponent if your Carbon Shinai is split or broken.

5. When tying the nakayui (leather binding), either tie a knot in the tsuru-ito (cord), or tie one end of the nakayui to the tsuru-ito, or by another means ensuring that is does not move up and down during use. If there is any damage whatsoever to the sakigawa, tsukagawa (hilt), rubber stopper, tsuru-ito and so on, replace them immediately.

6. If the tip of the Carbon Shinai is damaged, or a slat is protuding out of the sakigawa, there is a danger that it could enter your opponent's men grill and injure them.

Kendogu Revolution

Mu-Jun Men
武楯面

WARNING!!

1, Under no circumstances should organic solvents (such as thinner, alcohol, benzene, toluene, acetone, gasoline, kerosene, etc.), acidic or alkali chemicals, domestic cleansers, car cleansers, or anti-mist sprays, be used to clean the shield. These substances will cause the shield to deteriorate, leading to clouding, cracking or breaking, thereby resulting in danger of injury to the face.

2, Should the shield develop deep scratches or cracks on either the outer or inner surface, discontinue use of the shield immediately, and replace it with an undamaged shield. If the shield is used in such a condition, there is a danger of it breaking, causing injury to the face.

3, It should be fully understood that, as with the traditional Japanese Kendo-Men (mask), there is still the danger of injury to the face through fragments of broken bamboo or Carbon Shinai pieces penetrating through areas not covered by the shield.

SG-Type

- SCIENCE TO SEEK SAFETY -

HASEGAWA
HASEGAWA CORPORATION

WEB : http://kendo.hasegawakagaku.co.jp/
Email : contact@hasegawakagaku.co.jp

Carbon Shinai   Points to be checked

DANGER !!

ATTENTION !!

Before these happen.....

Although the Carbon Shinai is much more durable than a conventional bamboo one, it will inevitably become damaged since it is a sword that is used to repeatedly strike and thrust your opponent. Therefore, inspect the condition of the surface, sides or reverse of the Carbon Shinai's slats before, during and after use, and stop using it immediately should damage like in the following pictures be observed. (These pictures are just a few examples of many.)

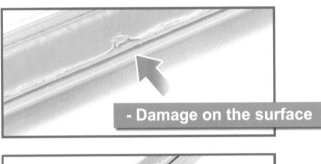

- Damage on the surface

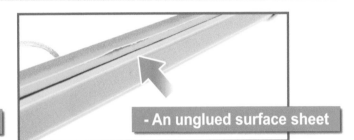

- An unglued surface sheet

- Exposure of the Carbon fiber

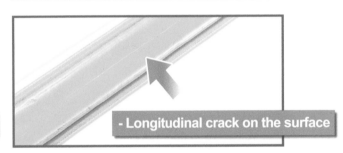

- Longitudinal crack on the surface

- Damage and ungluing of the surface

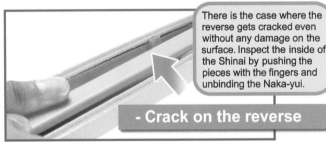

There is the case where the reverse gets cracked even without any damage on the surface. Inspect the inside of the Shinai by pushing the pieces with the fingers and unbinding the Naka-yui.

- Crack on the reverse

HASEGAWA-KOTE

- Detachable and washable "Tenouchi" is easy to wash and dry.

- "Tenouchi" is replaceable when torn. No need to repair.

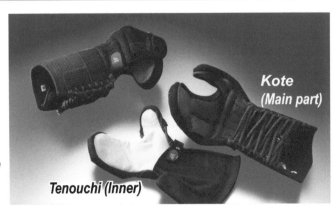

Kote (Main part)

Tenouchi (Inner)

- SCIENCE TO SEEK SAFETY -

HASEGAWA

HASEGAWA CORPORATION

http://kendo.hasegawakagaku.co.jp/

PUBLICATIONS

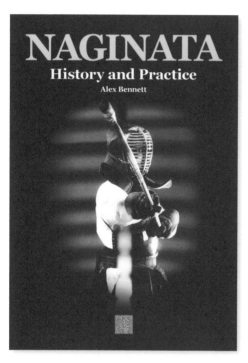

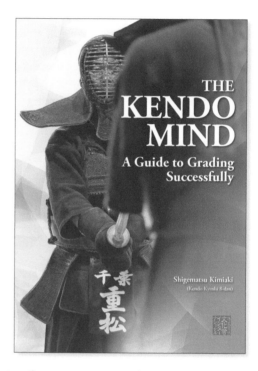

Naginata

Naginata, History and Practice

Of the handful of books on Naginata that do exist, most are prewar Japanese textbooks which are for the most part irrelevant to the popular form of Naginata developed in the post-war period. Postwar Naginata books are scant, and usually only cover the same basic techniques. Very little information is offered in regards to the cultural, historical, and mental aspects of Naginata. It requires a concerted effort to find such information in Japanese books, and to date, apart from a few journal articles, there has been virtually no work done in these areas in English or any other language. Until now, Naginata practitioners around the world have been left almost completely in the dark with regard to how the modern art that we practise today actually evolved and took its current form, in a process that spanned over one thousand years. This book fills the gap.

The Kendo Mind:

A Guide to Grading Successfully

Those who study kendo regard examinations and matches as vehicles for cultivating self-discipline and skill. Preparing to take a grading is especially motivating compared to regular training. It is, however, also a tremendous disappointment when you fail. There are those who manage to pass each examination without ever failing, and others who reach an impasse. So, what is the difference between these two groups? If you can figure it out, even just a little, you are one step closer to finding success. There are many things needed to pass an examination, not least of which is impressing the judges with resonating strikes. There is no way to achieve your goal without knowing how to accomplish this. The content of this book is based on lessons I learned from my sensei, my personal experiences in the dojo, and what I read in books and instruction manuals along the way. I hope that you will find the information in this small volume useful reference material as you navigate the path of kendo.

More info → www.kendo-world.com

KENDO WORLD Volume 8.4 March 2019 Contents

Kendo World Staff

◦Bunkasha International President & Editor-in-Chief— Alex Bennett PhD
◦Bunkasha International Vice President & Assistant Editor—Michael Ishimatsu-Prime MA
◦Bunkasha International Vice President & Graphic Design—Shishikura 'Kan' Masashi
◦Bunkasha International Vice President—Hamish Robison
◦Bunkasha International Vice President—Michael Komoto MA
◦Bunkasha International General Manager—Baptiste Tavernier MA
◦Senior Consultants—Yonemoto Masayuki, Shima Masahiko

KW Staff Writers | Translators | Photographers | Graphic Designer | Sub-editors

◦Axel Pilgrim PhD
◦Blake Bennett PhD
◦Bruce Flanagan MA
◦Bryan Peterson
◦Charlie Kondek
◦Gabriel Weitzner

◦Honda Sōtarō PhD
◦Imafuji Masahiro MBA
◦Jeff Broderick
◦Kate Sylvester PhD
◦Okuura Ayako
◦Sergio Boffa PhD

◦Stephen Nagy PhD
◦Steven Harwood MA
◦Takubo Seiya
◦Taylor Winter
◦Tony Cundy
◦Trevor Jones

◦Tyler Rothmar
◦Yamaguchi Remi
◦Vivian Yung
◦Yulin Zhuang

KW would like to thank the following people and organisations for their valuable cooperation:

◦All Japan Kendo Federation
◦Hasegawa Teiichi - President, Hasegawa Corporation
◦*Kendo Jidai* Magazine
◦*Kendo Nihon* Magazine

◦Nippon Budokan Foundation
◦Shogun Kendogu
◦TOZANDO

Guest Writers

◦Akos Vachter (Magyar-Japan Kendo Club, Hungary)
◦Clement Guo (UTS Kendo Club, Sydney)
◦Gabriel Weitzner (Kendo Renshi 7-dan, Canada)
◦Hatano Toshio (Kendo Kyōshi 8-dan)
◦HoJun Yoo (KW/Shogun Blue Label Article Comp. Winner)
◦James Ogle (Soft Tissue Therapist, Wellfield Osteopathy Clinic)
◦Jeff Marsten (Kendo Kyōshi 7-dan, PNKF)
◦Jo Anseeuw (Association for the Research and Preservation of Japanese Helmets and Armour)
◦Kusanagi Hiroki (Shogun Kendogu)
◦Ōya Minoru (Prof. International Budo University; Kendo Kyōshi 7-dan)
◦Shimokawa Mika (National Institute of Fitness and Sports in Kanoya)
◦Steve Hsueh (SCKO)
◦Takenaka Kentaro (National Institute of Fitness and Sports in Kanoya)
◦Zia Uddin (MWKF)

Editorial Conventions Used in KW Inevitably in a magazine of this nature, many non-English words appear in the text. All Japanese words are italicised and include macrons (ū, ō) etc., apart from common place names and nouns, and words in some captions and headings. As a general exception, KW treats all the martial arts (budo), such as kendo, iaido, jodo, ranks, and so on as Anglicised words without using macrons. Japanese names are written in accordance to the traditional Japanese manner of family name followed by given name. Traditional *ryūha* are written with capitals and therefore are not italicised. 'Kata' with a capital 'K' refers to the set of Nippon Kendo Kata, and *kata* refers to set forms in general. The masculine personal pronoun is used throughout the text in some articles in the interest of readability, and is in no way meant to slight the significant contributions made by female kendoka.

Editorial

Alex Bennett

Erai shitsurei shimashita. That's Kansai dialect for, "Begging your pardon folks…" It has been quite some time since the last issue of *Kendo World*. The blame rests solely on my shoulders. The past 18 months or so have been characterized by life sort of getting in the way. But KW is back, and we are on the verge of taking it to new heights. More on that later.

To start off, the Good Ship Kendo has been navigating choppy seas since we last published. Before commenting on the recent and much anticipated 17th WKC in Korea, I should begin with the "iaido debacle".

By now, details of the shocking revelations involving bribes to examiners in iaido 8-dan gradings have trickled through to the international community. Without going into too much detail, the AJKF recently conceded, after a thorough investigation following testimony by a whistle blower, that it had all but become customary for candidates of the coveted rank to offer examiners envelopes filled with cash. The whistle blower himself allegedly paid around 6,500,000-yen to realize his dream of becoming an iaido god. Evidently, no amount of money was enough to get him the required votes, and he threw his *katana* out of the cot. One could surmise that he must have been REALLY bad. One rather cynical observer pointed out that "he could have had 8-dan for much cheaper at one of the several 'lesser iaido organizations' that prey on disenfranchised AJKF iaido wannabes."

A number of Hanshi 8-dan sensei throughout the country were implicated, and an investigation to get to the bottom of this most un-budo-like fraud lifted a few weeping scabs. Handing over envelopes containing around 1,000,000-yen to *sensei* who were scheduled to sit on the grading panels "as a token of gratitude for their instruction" was a common method. Other sneaky means designed to placate their own tenuous consciences included selling a candidate a worthless sword for around 1,000,000-yen. There were also admissions of *ryūha* nepotism. In other words, an examiner from A-ryū would look favourably on fellow A-ryū disciples. All in all, such corruption had reached a level of endemic proportions, and the AJKF was swift to exorcise this evil spirit from its organization. The 8-dan examination for iaido was cancelled in May of 2017 as internal investigations were being held.

The upshot. Iaido examiners will remain anonymous until the day. The stipulation to do *koryū kata* in addition to AJKF iaido *kata* in 6-, 7-, and 8-dan examinations is now gone in Japan (for the meantime, but a travesty nonetheless for honest iaido diehards). The AJKF also imposed suspensions of membership and rank on the perpetrators, but those who admitted guilt in the allegations and "demonstrated remorse" were put on probation. The Beatles are also considering a new release of their old hit, "Can't buy me *hachi*."

But seriously folks, I was disturbed but not really surprised, at how serious this problem had become. I remember asking a friend around twenty years ago why there were so many courier trucks parked outside the iaido 8-dan examination venue. After all, nobody mails their *katana* home. "Well Alex, that's so that all of the examiners can send home the presents that candidates bring for them…"

It has always been there, and it has been that way for hundreds of years. Samurai were known to buy certification in such-and-such-ryū to prove to their bosses that they were still doing the samurai thing. The practice is still alive in many *kobudo* schools today. Iaido, being a *kata*-only budo, is prone to such problems because proficiency is so subjective. It's harder to justify passing somebody in a kendo examination if s/he gets smashed all over the floor.

Even though this happened a few years ago, the Japanese media jumped on it in August 2017. I was dismayed to read the headlines in the *Japan Times* about the dismal affair. "The martial art of kendo has been hit by its own corruption scandal, with the All Japan Kendo Federation saying Friday that people taking promotional exams often paid money to their examiners in order to win their approval." (JT Aug. 17, 2018) Fortunately, "kendo" was amended to "iaido" in the online edition on August 29, but it is not a good look for the federation and detracts from the incredible dedication and hard work that genuine stalwarts of either art put into their study.

These days, there seems to be a media feeding frenzy every week regarding some untoward goings on in the sports world in Japan. American football, boxing, iaido, gymnastics… Maybe it is a good thing to clean a few skeletons out of changing room lockers as Japan gears up to host the world's premium sporting event in Tokyo in 2020. Then again, if ever there was a toxic carcinogen to the spirit of sport, the "Five Rings" would be it… I am not talking about Miyamoto Musashi. In any case, good luck karate. You're going to need it more than ever following your 2020 Olympic debut.

Erai shitsurei shimashita… Here I go again. Preaching in "holier-than-thou" tones about the spirit of budo and kendo. Oh, we *kendoka* are so good, aren't we? The 17th WKC was held for the first time in Korea in 30 years in September 2018. The last time the WKC was held in Korea was way back in 1988 in Seoul. There is a good reason for this 30-year hiatus. During the usual tight contest in the men's team final between Korea and Japan, the referees were perceived by the Korean spectators as being somewhat biased. I wasn't there and cannot comment on the veracity of such claims. The point is, the arena erupted into a fissure spewing molten discord in the form of bottles being thrown from the bleachers at the officials below. The Shinpan and competitors had to be escorted from the venue for their own safety.

This time I wondered how things would pan out. Obviously, Korea has long wanted to put this ghost to bed, but at the same time, desperately want to defeat the Japanese for the first time. Oh, how close they have been over the years. The greatest opportunity to defeat their nemesis on home soil awaited the Korean team.

Tickets for the event mysteriously sold out quicker than the latest Beatles single "Can't buy me *hachi*". It seemed that only Koreans had a chance to purchase tickets to the 8000-person venue. The rest of the world had little chance to get their share of Willy Wonker's little gold tickets. Friends in Japan said they didn't care. "It was going to be a shambles anyway." "Besides," I was told by one friend, "The Korean right-wing hooligans are rumoured to have bought up all the tickets, so a repeat of 1988 is on the cards again…"

Honestly speaking, I was relieved to be going as the head coach of NZ, thanking the kendo gods I was not a Shinpan… I translated at the WKC Shinpan seminar held in Narita in June and know all the *sensei* who were tasked with this potentially volatile mission. But then again, as extolled in that old Bushido classic, *Hagakure*, "The more it rains, the higher the boat floats." Indeed, this was going to be another test of how durable kendo has become in the ocean of globalisation. After all, the point of kendo is to take us all out of our comfort zone and test us in the cauldron of adversity.

The 17th WKC was as predicted, a feisty affair. There were a few upsets and near upsets along the way in the Men's and Women's individual and team competitions. Vivid in my memory is the semi-final match between the French and Korean men. For a moment I thought that Korea were going to be defeated on their home turf before they got the chance to have a crack at Japan. The local crowd was appreciative of the dazzling display of fighting spirit demonstrated by the French, taking their team down to the wire.

The Japanese women proved to be in a league of their own the day before. Nobody was really sure what would happen in the final of the men's team competition. It worked out to be yet another classic Japan-Korea encounter. All the videos are available for viewing on Kendo World's YouTube page, so I will not bore you with a commentary here. Suffice it to say, when the Japanese Taisho survived the onslaught of his Korean counterpart to clinch victory for Japan's sixteenth world title, the hitherto vociferous crowd poured out of Incheon's Namdong Gymnasium in stunned silence. To say they were "frustrated" is probably a gross understatement.

Now, where are we here at Kendo World? Since 2001 when we were first started by a couple of totally inexperienced Kiwi lads who just loved living the dream hitting people with sticks in Japan, the magazine has been a work in progress. The group of dedicated kendo bums who chose to jump on for the ride have kept it going through thick and thin, riding the ebbs and flows and balancing precariously on a tightrope separating our real lives and what we would rather be doing. It has almost been 20 years now, and somehow, almost miraculously I would say, we have kept KW afloat through pure doggedness and our passion for kendo. This has been possible through adapting to and adopting the ever-changing technology that has revolutionized publishing and the dissemination of information.

Compared to 20 years ago it is implausibly easy to access information in kendo and the related arts. Gone are the days of sending a grainy VHS recording of the All Japan Kendo Championships back to hankering kendo buddies in NZ or Australia. Just watch the AJKF stream, or go onto YouTube to get ringside seats. All federations have their own websites now, and Facebook and other social media platforms have us all linked together. Our Kendo World Forum served a wonderful purpose in its day but is mostly irrelevant now.

Like any undertaking in any field, to lose relevance is the death knoll and time to retire. We all know, however, that there is no retirement in kendo. As the adage goes, "Kendoka never die, they just smell that way." Kendo World has no intention of dying either. To this end, once again, we are completely redoing our format.

There is a hybrid English word used in Japanese called "Mook". It means "Magazine-Book". From now, instead of a potpourri of kendo information from events around the world, happenings in Japan, miscellaneous interviews with *sensei*, and so on, Kendo World will be published as a Mook which focuses closely on a particular subject rather than a miscellany of topics. This KW issue being No. 4 of Volume 8 will be the last in this format. Our next publication which we aim to have out *sometime in 2019* will be KW 9.1 (as with our usual numbering format) but the content will focus on the theme of *"seme"*.

Furthermore, Kendo World has started up a Patreon page. This is an exciting point in our evolution. The goal of Kendo World has never been to get rich. From the start, it has always been to provide the international kendo community with relevant, useful, and accurate information on kendo and related arts utilising our strong network of enthusiasts and *sensei* in Japan and around the world. Running costs, however, are a fact of life. Patreon provides a platform which enables us to convey even more kendo information, on time, and to the point. We sincerely hope that you will continue to support Kendo World as we try to support you.

Uncle Kotay's Kendo Korner

Part 4:
Win Before You Strike!

Q: Hey Uncle Kotay, I'm sorry to always keep bugging you, but I've got another question. In a shiai the other day, I thought I had the perfect opportunity so I tried to strike my opponent's men. However, my opponent instantly blocked me and scored ippon with men-kaeshi-do! I ended up losing the match, and afterwards one of my senpai said to me, "You need to win before you strike!" That seemed a bit back the front. Surely you strike to win? Can you tell me what he means? (#confusedagain)

A: Well, that was actually some very good advice. In Japanese, there is an expression "*katte-utsu*" (勝って打つ: win and then strike), and. It refers to the work or preparation that you need to do **_before_** you attempt a strike. In your *shiai* it sounds like you didn't prepare properly before striking your opponent. In other words, you hadn't created the opportunity. Another reason for your loss could be that your opponent enticed you into striking before you were ready, thus creating an opportunity for him. He won the encounter before he struck.

To create an opening against your opponent, you need to apply *seme*. For example, gradually move in from *tōma* to *issoku-ittō-no-maai*. From there, quickly take a half step forward with the right foot to move into *chika-ma*. If your opponent is resolute and holds still, their *kensen* still pointing at your throat, don't attack. You need to regroup and continue on to your next strategy. If your opponent flinches, takes a step back, or maybe raises their hands, you have created the opportunity which should be grabbed immediately.

Of course, the strike needs to be made with *ki-ken-tai-itchi*, and you must show *zanshin* afterwards for it to be judged *ippon*.

You don't win because you strike your opponent; you strike your opponent because you have already won.

Those fantastic guys at *Kendo World* captured an amazing contest between Sakudō Masao-sensei and Hamasaki Mitsuru-sensei, both Hanshi 8-dan, at the 109th Kyoto Taikai in 2013. It was a match that epitomised *katte-utsu*. For the entire bout, neither sensei made a strike. Both stood in *chudan-no-kamae* trying to control the centre. When one moved forward, the other held firm or controlled the opponent's *shinai*. Neither could create a clear-cut opportunity to strike, so neither did. The control demonstrated by both sensei to hold on, maintain their composure and not be rushed into making a strike was truly amazing. The video is named "109th Kyoto Taikai - Sakudo / Hamasaki" and can be found on the Kendo World YouTube channel. You really should watch it.

So, the next time that you are doing *ji-geiko* or you're in a competition, don't just charge in willy-nilly. Try to beat your opponent **_before_** you strike them. This isn't going to be easy, and it will take a lot of practice, but as the old adage states, hard practice makes hard-ass kendo machines.

Kendo and the Human Condition

KENDO WORLD / SHOGUN KENDOGU BLUE LABEL ARTICLE COMPETITION WINNER!

HoJun Yoo

HoJun Yoo (far right)

"I don't want to see anyone. I lie in the bedroom with the curtains drawn and nothingness washing over me like a sluggish wave. Whatever is happening to me is my own fault. I have done something wrong, something so huge I can't even see it, something that's drowning me. I am inadequate and stupid, without worth. I might as well be dead."

Margaret Atwood, "Cat's Eye"

Winter, 2013

Feeling utterly broken, I sit on the edge of my bed, surrounded by the suffocating darkness and silence. The clock reads four in the afternoon, and the winter sun should be about to set soon, but I can only guess. I haven't been outside in over a week. Looking around the spartan room, I feel utterly detached, though the detachment is better than the usual crushing sense of self-loathing, panic, and anxiety. It is as close to relief as I can get.

An hour passes in the darkness. My phone vibrates; a video call from my grandfather. It's 5pm now, only 7am in Korea, far too early for him to be calling, especially on a Saturday morning, which is when he usually goes for a walk to the local temple. There's no need to get him worried. I decide to turn the lights on and answer the call, trying to put on my best "I'm fine" face.

He doesn't ask about school or my hospital work. Instead, he asks me about whether I've been to kendo lately. I say "no". He doesn't ask why. He never does. He just says that he wishes I would pick it up again. "You've been doing it since you were nine! You haven't gotten your 3-dan yet, right?" (At that point in my life, he was right. It had been seven years since I had passed my 2-dan grading.) Knowing it's something he's proud of, I promise to get back to it. He seems placated, and we wave good-bye.

Shutting the lights off again, I lie back down on the bed. Since it is a Friday when the college kendo club holds practices, I figure I might as well go. Surprisingly, I actually get up. Turning the lights back on, I shuffle over to the closet, where my *bōgu* and *shinai* have been stuffed for the last two years.

* * * *

I struggled with depression and overall psychological health since my early youth. It had no origin, no big life changing event I could attribute it to, nothing I could blame. It came without warning and crushed me, a silent and oppressive monster that refused to leave. When I mentioned it to anybody else, I was guaranteed a variation of one of three responses:

"Things will get better."
"Pull it together."
"Just think positively and cheer up!"

I learned early on that it was better to not speak of it to others. So it stayed, a silent and invisible malady. Throughout this lifelong ordeal, kendo occupied a curious position in my life. Having practised kendo since I turned ten years old, it was a constant presence. It was just something that I did, like my friends who played basketball or soccer or a musical instrument. I never gave the role that kendo played in my life much thought until that fateful day in college, when my grandfather called.

Since that day, kendo has become an essential component of my life. It was a habit I sought for refuge when I was mired in the depths of my depression. It provided me with lessons, fortifying me with hope and confidence. It served as a parallel to life from which I was able to learn from. As I've grown and matured, kendo has functioned and adapted to a variety of roles, and it has been crucial to my recovery. Naturally, I began to think about kendo as it relates to my psychological well-being. What about it resonated with me so profoundly? I grew up hearing about how martial arts would make me "mentally strong", but I was not interested in that. I was interested in why kendo made me feel "well", why it gave me a sense of well-being that felt transferable to my everyday life, why it made me feel alive.

One of the most widely accepted models on psychological well-being is Professor Carol D. Ryff's six-factor model[1]. Here, a person scores themselves on six criteria, where a high score has been shown to be a reliable indicator of a person's well-being. These criteria are:

1. Self-acceptance
2. Environmental mastery
3. Autonomy
4. Personal growth
5. Purpose in life/pursuit of meaningful goals
6. Positive relations with others

Reflecting upon these six qualities, it struck me as remarkable was how applicable they were to my own experiences in kendo. It provided an elegant framework to reflect on why kendo had been such a positive and meaningful experience for me.

Take, for example, the criteria of self-acceptance. Self-acceptance is the acceptance of multiple aspects of oneself, requiring not only embracing of the positive, but also acknowledgement of the negative. It is the ability to view the self as a whole being, with all the imperfections, talents, deficiencies, and assets that being a human entails. It is a thoroughly *wabi-sabi*-esque perspective on oneself. What is important here is that in order to be self-accepting, one must first be self-aware. In kendo, this self-awareness is an essential component of our training, as it allows us to see with clarity what we can and cannot do. This awareness helps allay the frustrations and it can help us change our perspective to focus on our potential. It shows us what we can improve on, provide us with goals, and allow us to perform to the best of our abilities. Self-acceptance, in short, provides us with the wisdom to seek improvement, rather than perfection.

Then, there is environmental mastery in which a high scorer is somebody who "has a sense of mastery and competence in managing the environment; controls complex array of external activities; makes effective use of surrounding opportunities; able to choose or create contexts suitable to personal needs and values".[2] While it is undeniably true that there are numerous external factors which we have no control over, it does

1 Ryff, Carol D. "Happiness is everything, or is it? Explorations on the meaning of psychological well-being." *Journal of Personality and Social Psychology*, vol. 57, no. 6, 1989, pp. 1069–1081., doi:10.1037//0022-3514.57.6.1069.

2 *Ibid.*

not mean that we are helpless. What is important is the management and utilization of that environment. In kendo, we seek to achieve this environmental mastery by creating and taking advantage of opportunities via the manipulation of the opponent's fighting spirit, body, and sword, utilising such concepts as *seme* and *tame*. We can make our opponents afraid to commit and position ourselves to be in a superior state of readiness. Although we cannot stop the opponent from attacking, we can utilise it as an opening; every attack by the opponent can be countered – a *men* becomes *men-kaeshi-dō*, *debana-kote*, or even *ai-men*.

Yet just as we seek to exert our influence upon the opponent, so too does the other seek to do the same to us. While there are numerous definitions of autonomy, Ryff defines it as the state where one "is self-determining and independent; able to resist social pressures to think and act in certain ways; regulates behaviour from within; evaluates self by personal standards".[3] Similarly, kendo practitioners strive to hold the centre and perform to their own ideals of kendo, even when under environmental pressure, such as the pressure applied by their opponent, the pressure of tournaments or gradings, and even the pressure players often place upon themselves. In *keiko*, we try to put ourselves in a favourable position in order to execute our *waza*. Such is the case when we pressure *men* and switch it up to a *kote* when the opponent raises their *shinai*. Similarly, we seek to do the same to ourselves and override this natural instinct to retreat and block half-heartedly.

The cultivation of these three factors are not independent of each other. Through self-acceptance, we glean the self-awareness necessary to inform us how we can better master our environment and maintain our autonomy. This requires of us the clarity to see both our strengths and flaws and the humility to accept them. It requires us to observe, with a keen eye, the environment, to see what we can and cannot change, and how we can take advantage of it. It allows us to hold true to ourselves and our capabilities, the insight to play *our* game, not the opponent's. As

Sun Tzu wrote, "If you know the enemy and know yourself, you need not fear the result of a hundred battles."

The next two criteria, that of personal growth and the pursuit of meaningful goals, are the very embodiment of kendo. Here personal growth is defined as when one "has a feeling of continued development; sees self as growing and expanding…changing in ways that reflect more self-knowledge and effectiveness",[4] and those with a purpose in life as those who are pursuing meaningful goals. Without purpose and growth, both human existence and kendo can feel inconsequential—I certainly felt that way about my life. But this is a stagnant and barren view, for they are both infinitely complex and indeed, infinite. That there is no "goal", no pinnacle, or no objective "end-point", speaks volumes about the boundless possibilities of both life and kendo. There is always room for growth and development, always new experiences to be had, and the journey itself provides the meaning. Every goal that we accomplish provides us with another goal to be pursued. In both kendo and life, I have found that fulfilment lies in the process and the meaningfulness I ascribe to them. Truly, "the devil is in the details, but so is salvation".[5]

Finally, kendo is impossible without the final criteria, that of positive relationships with others. The very making of a *kenshi* is a community effort. There are the *sensei* and *senpai* to guide us, fellow *kenshi* to practise with, the *motodachi* who sacrifice their forearms, armpits, and necks for us, and even other *dōjō* to compete with. The communal goal is the transference of knowledge, on mutual development. Consider, additionally, the fact that when a *kenshi* achieves the rank of 4-dan, we call her *sensei*, meaning teacher. What is expected of her is not exceptional kendo, but the cultivation of others' kendo. These expectations are mutual. We thank our *sensei* and *senpai*, not only for their knowledge, but for their time and effort. We thank them for their empathy because they know our toils, having seen others go

---

3 *Ibid.*

4 *Ibid.*

5 Hyman G. Rickover

through the same process, and having gone through it themselves. We thank our opponents and practice partners. We thank each other for practice and advice. This ideal is the *rei* of kendo.

By no means am I attempting to equate kendo with life. Neither are capable of being so simplified. In applying Ryff's criteria for everyday psychological well-being in the capacity of kendo, I have simply attempted to draw the parallels that I've seen between the two as they apply to my experiences. Perhaps there is some transference of these aspects of kendo to everyday life. I'd like to think so. But for me, kendo plays a further role, one I deem more personally important—that of a haven.

* * * *

I still remember my first practice back. Although it had been years, I was greeted warmly by the *sensei* and club members. Most of the old guard had graduated, but there were a few familiar faces. As we ran through the stretches and *kihon*, I felt my body groaning, forced to move in ways it had not in months. I gradually felt my old instincts return, the old, dry *shinai* feeling familiar in my hands.

After practice, sitting in *seiza*, quads and back already sore from the sudden work they had not been forced to do in ages, I felt—truly felt—my body: my lungs filling with air, blood rushing through my legs and shoulders and back, the welts from mishit kote throbbing, my throat aching, and my heart pounding. There was also a numbness that settled my mind. It was different from the normal anaesthetic numbness that sedated my mind. It wasn't white noise that drowned out internal discordance, but a serene silence. It was the kind of numbness that came from freeing the body, losing oneself in the endless repetition of *kihon* and *keiko*, not the numbness that comes from the crushing claustrophobia of being entombed within one's own mind. The usually numbing overflow of mental processes was temporarily replaced by silence. It was my rudimentary glimpse into the state of *mushin*, if you will.

Grandpa and me

I surprised my grandfather by calling him after practice that night. He didn't comment too much on it, as he seemed to sense that I just needed to let him know that I had done something, however insignificant that thing might be. After that, I kept going to practice. It became a routine, a part of my everyday life that helped anchor me during times of tumult and personal strife.

My struggle with my mental well-being continued—continues—to this day. It is a chronic condition; an untamed condition not to be conquered, but understood and endured. When I struggled to keep my head above the inexorable waves, like a person stranded in the middle of the ocean in a typhoon, kendo gave me a way to keep myself grounded. But in another way, kendo is my melancholy come alive—my depression, self-doubt, and anxiety—physically manifested for me to overcome. Through kendo, I understood that just as the mind was an escape for physical pain, so too could the body be an escape from mental pain. Kendo is all that, and more. It is my community, the pre-practice chats while stretching and stomping lightly on the ground, warming up the soles of our feet for *fumikomi*. It is the post-practice hangouts and the long drives with sensei and friends to far-away tournaments. It is a driver of my education and growth as a kenshi and person, my self-acceptance. Most importantly, it is a phone call from a loving grandfather to a young man trapped inside his own mind in a dark room. It may just be kendo, but it provides me with the courage and hope to take on another day.

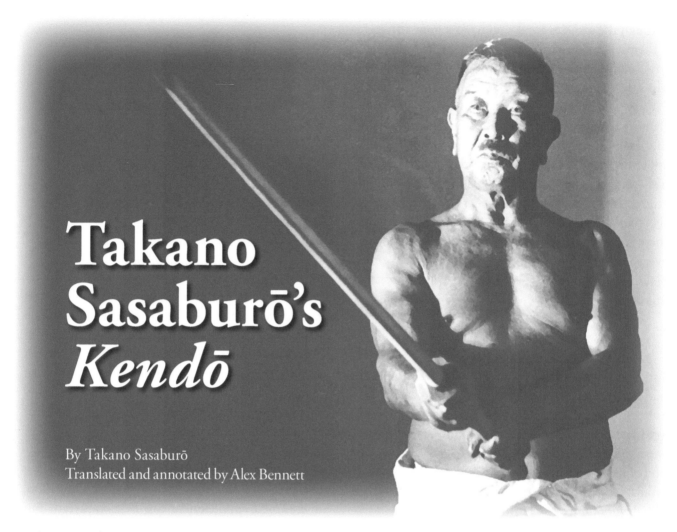

Takano Sasaburō's *Kendō*

By Takano Sasaburō
Translated and annotated by Alex Bennett

Takano Sasaburō (1862–1950) is considered one of the most influential pioneers of modern kendo. He was instrumental in developing the *dan* grading system for kendo and was also a key member in the committee that created the Kendo Kata in 1912. His book, simply titled *Kendō*, was a tour de force in the creation of a uniform style for modern kendo and is still considered a classic by kendoka today. In this series of articles, I will translate Takano's book, and annotate the text to add context to its ground-breaking content. The following is the last sections of Chapter 3 of *Kendō*.

Kata

Kata forms were created by selecting the most fundamental techniques in kendo. Through studying *kata*, students develop good posture, hone their power of observation, fix bad technical habits, learn the correct cutting angle of the blade, become more agile and lighter in movement, develop precise striking technique, understand correct distancing (*maai*), improve their temperament, and augment a strong spirit (*kiai*). It is for these reasons that *kata* practice is crucial. If students were to don equipment and engage in competitive bouts from the outset, their posture and movements will become distorted, they will become impervious to matters of *kiai* and *maai*, and their striking will become flawed. Many problems would arise, and progress will be slow as a result. Therefore, in the old days it was necessary to learn *kata* thoroughly before progressing on to competitive matches. Once the basic actions are mastered, students should be suitably instructed in the subtleties of *kata*.

Demonstrations of *kata* should be executed conscientiously and with ample fighting spirit, with vigilance, and in one unbroken breath in line with the principles of swordsmanship. In *kata*, not only form is important but so is the spirit in which it is executed. If spirit is lacking and the performance is careless, it degrades into little more than a dance or exercise without real substance.

In the first year of Taisho (1912), the Greater Japan Martial Virtue Society (Dai-Nippon Butokukai)[1] collaborated with the Tokyo Higher Normal School to formulate the "Greater Japan Imperial Kendo Kata."[2] There were hundreds of *kata* forms in the various classical schools of swordsmanship. Oftentimes these forms were outdated and unsuitable for teaching in modern kendo.

The "Greater Japan Imperial Kendo Kata" were created by lead investigators Naitō Takaharu, Monna Tadashi, Negishi Shingorō of Tokyo, and Tsuji Shinpei of Kyushu, and myself making five in total.[3] Experts from around the country were consulted and suitable techniques were incorporated into the set of *kata*. With the completion of the Greater Japan Imperial Kendo Kata, previous sets developed by the Butokukai and the Ministry of Education were discarded.[4]

Many conventional forms were practised only as *kata* and had little practical application in bouts. Ten forms were created in total, and they were designed to lead into techniques for application in competitive bouts. The following is an outline of the *kata*. The explanations are somewhat streamlined, so I will add further details when necessary.

Greater-Japan Imperial Kendo Kata

Tachiai

• Both Uchidachi and Shidachi hold their swords at the side (*sagetō* position) and commence with a standing mutual bow of respect.

• The starting distance between Uchidachi and Shidachi (*tachi maai*) is approximately nine-paces (5.4 metres) apart. After the bow, both proceed three steps forward and draw swords out together as they crouch down into *sonkyo*. Both stand up into the fighting stance (*kamae*) in the natural standing posture moving the right foot slightly forward, the tips of the swords are lowered, and then both retreat

five steps from the left foot.

• The final bow is performed in the same way as the first one.

Explanation

In the *kata*, Shidachi takes the central role while Uchidachi facilitates. Shidachi must move according to his own will, whereas Uchidachi is supposed to aid. As both advance three steps, the interval reached is also three steps apart, the optimal distance. Swords are drawn and crossed while going down into *sonkyo*. Then both stand and retreat the distance covered in three steps with five small steps back, ending up in a position nine paces apart. At this point, Shidachi steps forward with the right foot and assumes two-handed right *jōdan*. Uchidachi steps back with the right foot and assumes two-handed left *jōdan*.[5] Both Uchidachi and Shidachi are primed to take the initiative.

Kakegoe (Yell)

• The two yells are *yaa* and *toh*.

Sword

• Use naked blades (*shiraha*) on formal occasions.

• Use wooden swords (*bokutō*) when practising. The length of the *bokutō* is 101.5cm, of which the handle (*tsuka*) is 24.24cm with 1.5cm between the *tsuba* (hand guard) and the *seppa* (thin washers on either side of the *tsuba*). The *kodachi* is 54.5cm in length, with the *tsuka* measuring 13.3cm.

About to draw the sword *Sagetō position*

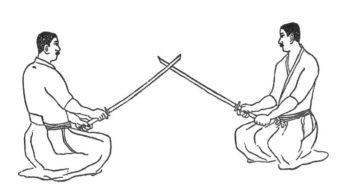

Swords drawn at sonkyo

Kensen lowered before moving back to starting positions

Dai-ippon (No. 1)

Both advance with Uchidachi in *hidari-morote-jōdan* and Shidachi in the *migi-morote-jōdan* stance. (Uchidachi steps forward from the left foot and Shidachi from the right.) Upon reaching the interval for engagement, Uchidachi looks for the right opportunity and timing and then steps forward from the right foot to strike Shidachi's *shōmen*. Shidachi moves slightly back from the left foot [to avoid the strike] and then attacks Uchidachi's *shōmen*. Shidachi demonstrates *zanshin* by stepping forward with the left foot and assuming [*hidari-morote-*] *jōdan*. With the *kensen* still lowered in the *gedan* position, Uchidachi takes two small steps back and then lifts the *kensen* up into *chūdan*. At the same time, Shidachi brings the sword down from *jōdan* to meet in *chūdan*. Both lower their swords and return to the start positions.

Explanation

Both advance confidently. When the interval for engagement is reached, Uchidachi applies pressure on Shidachi. Upon identifying a chance to strike Uchidachi unleashes an attack to Shidachi's *shōmen* and *tsuka* of the sword. Shidachi takes a small step back from the left foot to avoid the strike and then counterattacks Uchidachi's *shōmen* taking advantage of his unbalanced posture. Shidachi wins with the timing of *sen-sen-no-sen* (counterattacking the opponent while they are attacking). Shidachi then steps forward with the left foot into *jōdan* to demonstrate a continued state of vigilance (*zanshin*). From the

initial strike to taking *jōdan*, Shidachi must be ready to attack again should Uchidachi make even the slightest move.

Dai-nihon (No. 2)

Both Uchidachi and Shidachi advance toward each other in *chūdan*. When the interval for engagement is reached, Uchidachi seizes the opportunity to strike at right *kote*. Shidachi moves to the left from the left foot followed by the right. Taking a big step in from the right foot, Shidachi strikes Uchidachi's righ-*kote*. Both then assume the *chūdan* stance, lower *kensen*, and return to the starting positions.

Explanation

Both advance confidently in *ai-chūdan*. When the correct interval is reached, Uchidachi looks for the opportunity and attacks right-*kote*. Shidachi avoids the strike by moving to the side from the left then right foot, and then takes a big step in with the right foot to strike Uchidachi's right *kote* winning with the *sen-sen-no-sen* timing. From here, Shidachi demonstrates *zanshin* as both return to *chūdan*. Shidachi must keep the pressure on Uchidachi and be ready to strike again at any given moment.

Dai-sanbon (No. 3)

Both Uchidachi and Shidachi assume *gedan* and advance from the right foot. Upon reaching the interval for engagement, Uchidachi seizes the opportunity by twisting the blade to the left of Shidachi's sword and thrusting with both hands to

Shidachi's chest. Shidachi absorbs the momentum of the thrust rendering it ineffective, and thrusts back at Uchidachi's chest. Uchidachi steps back from the right foot pressing Shidachi's *kensen* to the right, then steps back with the left foot pressing the *kensen* to the left. Shidachi pushes forward from the left then right foot, and then takes two or three steps from the right foot to force Uchidachi back. Both assume *chūdan* and return to the centre, then lower the *kensen* before returning to the start positions.

Explanation

Both advance confidently in the *gedan* posture. When the interval for engagement is reached, Uchidachi and Shidachi are primed to clash. The *kensen* are raised at the same time from *gedan* into *chūdan*. At that point, Uchidachi seizes the opportunity and thrusts at Shidachi's chest. Shidachi, with a feeling of "rock over cloth" averts the thrust while at the same time, and with resolve as steady as a rock, returns a thrust to Uchidachi's chest to win with the timing of *sen-sen-no-sen*. Shidachi demonstrates replete *zanshin* and keeps the pressure on Uchidachi.

Dai-yonhon (No. 4)

Uchidachi from *hassō* and Shidachi from *wakigamae* advance toward each other from the left foot. When the interval for engagement is reached, Uchidachi seizes the opportunity and strikes at Shidachi's *shōmen*. At the same time, Shidachi attacks Uchidachi's *shōmen* from *wakigamae* so that the swords meet in a concurrent strike. Uchidachi turns the blade slightly to Shidachi's left and stepping out with the right foot thrusts with both hands at Shidachi's chest. Shidachi pivots on the left foot to the left, deflects the thrust and follows with a strike to *men*. Both return to *chūdan*, lower *kensen*, and return to starting positions.

Explanation

Uchidachi takes the *hassō* posture and Shidachi assumes *wakigamae*. *Hassō* is not the aggressor in this case but yields to *wakigamae*. *Wakigamae* is referred to as the "metal" stance, as if one has gold in his pocket but this is not revealed to the opponent and is used only when the circumstance calls for it. It is a posture that can adapt to various situations.

The will of Shidachi, therefore, is concealed from Uchidachi, and changes depending on Uchidachi's actions. As it is stated in the outline, when the interval for engagement has been reached, both seize the opportunity to aim for the bridge of the nose in a big cut. The cuts are simultaneous and the sides of the swords (*shinogi*) grind together and the left foot is moved back to the launching distance as both assume *chūdan*. Uchidachi suppresses Shidachi's sword and binds it as he thrusts at the chest. Shidachi uses Uchidachi's thrusting power and prevails by bringing the left foot to the left side while avoiding (*nuki*) the thrust then striking *men* as the right foot is brought behind the left. The timing of the victory is *go-no-sen*. Demonstrate *zanshin*.

Dai-gohon (No. 5)

Uchidachi assumes *hidari-morote-jōdan* and Shidachi takes *seigan* (*chūdan*) and both advance (Uchidachi from the left foot, and Shidachi from the right). Upon reaching the interval for engagement Uchidachi seizes the opportunity, and stepping out with the right foot, strikes Shidachi's *men* from *morote-jōdan*. Shidachi parries the attack up (*suriage*) and strikes Uchidachi's *men*. Then, pulling back the right foot, assumes *hidari-jōdan* and demonstrates *zanshin*. The sword is brought down, and both return to starting positions.

Explanation

From *jōdan* and *seigan*, both advance confidently. Seizing the opportunity, Uchidachi strikes at Shidachi's *men*. Shidachi steps back from the left followed by the right while lifting the sword up to parry (*suriage*) Uchidachi's attack and wins with *go-no-sen* timing.

Dai-roppon (No. 6)

Uchidachi assumes *seigan*, and Shidachi *gedan*. Both advance from the right foot. When the interval for engagement is reached, Shidachi seizes the opportunity and raises the tip of the sword into the *seigan* position. Uchidachi pulls the right foot back and simultaneously assumes *hidari jōdan*. Staying in *seigan*, Shidachi takes a big step forward with the right foot. Uchidachi immediately returns to *seigan*, seizes the opportunity, and immediately strikes right *kote*. Shidachi deflects the strike upwards with *suriage* while shifting the left foot to the left and stepping in with the right foot to strike right *kote*. Shidachi then steps out with the left foot and assumes *jōdan* to demonstrate *zanshin*. Uchidachi lowers *kensen* and steps back a little from the left foot. Both assume *ai-seigan*, lower the *kensen*, and return to starting positions.

Explanation

From *seigan* and *gedan*, both advance with confidence. As Shidachi lifts from *gedan* to *seigan*, Uchidachi evades by lifting back into *jōdan*. Shidachi simultaneously takes a step forward. Unable to withstand the pressure, Uchidachi steps back from the left foot and assumes *chūdan*. It appears Shidachi is about to take another step forward to attack so Uchidachi makes a small *de-gote* strike. Shidachi shifts the left foot to the left and steps forward from the right while executing *suriage* to deflect the incoming technique to strike *kote* winning with *go-no-sen*. Shidachi then assumes *jōdan* to demonstrate *zanshin* and check Uchidachi with a continued attacking spirit.

Dai-nanahon (No. 7)

From *seigan* Uchidachi and Shidachi advance from the right foot. When the interval for engagement is reached, Uchidachi seizes the moment and thrusts at Shidachi's chest with both hands. Shidachi extends both hands and curbs the incoming sword. Both assume the *seigan* position. Uchidachi then steps forward from the left foot and then the right throwing their whole body into a strike to Shidachi's *men*. Shidachi shifts the right foot to the right, and then moves the left foot to evade the incoming attack while striking right-*dō* with both hands. The right knee touches the floor as Shidachi assumes *sonkyo wakigamae* to demonstrate *zanshin*. Both assume *ai-seigan*, lower the *kensen*, and return to start positions.

Explanation

From *ai-seigan*, Uchidachi and Shidachi advance with confidence. Shidachi receives Uchidachi's thrust as explained above and both swords rise. As both go down into *chūdan*, Uchidachi attacks Shidachi's *shōmen*. As explained, Shidachi strikes Uchidachi's right-*dō* winning by *go-no-sen*, then demonstrates *zanshin* in a show of dominance.

Kodachi-no-Kata
(Uchidachi= Long Sword, Shidachi = Short Sword)

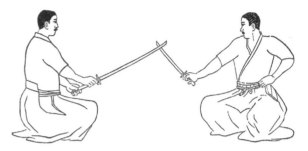

Swords drawn in sonkyo position

Standing posture after drawing swords

Lowering kensen to move back to starting positions

Kodachi fudō no shisei
(posture of the immovable kodachi)

Dai-ippon (No. 1)

Uchidachi assumes *jōdan* and Shidachi *seigan hanmi-no-kamae*. Both advance toward each other (Uchidachi from the left foot and Shidachi from the right). As Shidachi leans forward (*irimi*) to advance, Uchidachi moves forward in *jōdan* and seizes the opportunity to strike down at Shidachi's *shōmen*. Shidachi shifts to the diagonal right while deflecting the incoming blow and then strikes Uchidachi's *shōmen*. Taking a big step back from the left foot Shidachi assumes *jōdan* to demonstrate *zanshin*. Both assume *ai-chūdan*, lower their *kensen* and return to starting positions.

As Uchidachi changes to *seigan*, Shidachi suppresses this and moves in (*irimi*). Uchidachi then swings back into *wakigamae*. Shidachi moves in close again (*irimi*) and Uchidachi strikes at *shōmen* from *wakigamae*. Shidachi moves the left foot forward to the diagonal left and pivots to the left while deflecting the strike down (*ukenagashi*) and strikes *men*. Shidachi then grabs Uchidachi's upper arm and points the *kensen* at Uchidachi's throat to demonstrate *zanshin*. Then both assume *seigan*, lower the *kensen*, and return to the start positions

Kodachi seigan hanmi (against jōdan)

Kodachi seigan hanmi (against gedan)

Explanation

The wielder of the *kodachi* must have a feeling that they are not in possession of a weapon, and should not think to stave off Uchidachi's sword or of winning. Uchidachi takes *jōdan*, and Shidachi assumes a *hanmi* stance from *seigan* with the right arm adequately extended with the *kensen* at nose height. Taking this posture allows the *kodachi* to compensate for the length of the longer sword. Both advance. As Uchidachi strikes down at *shōmen* Shidachi shifts to the diagonal right while receiving the incoming blade to deflect it, not block it. The *kodachi* will snap if it is not averted downwards. This *kata* is also called "essential form" (*shin no kata*).[6] Shidachi must be of the mind to dispatch Uchidachi immediately with no hesitation.

Dai-nihon (No. 2)

Uchidachi assumes *gedan* and Shidachi takes *seigan hanmi-no-kamae*. Both advance from the right foot.

Explanation

This form is also called "*gyō no kata*". Shidachi does not attempt to dispatch Uchidachi straight away. Shidachi should be of the mind not to submit to Uchidachi's will, but to take Uchidachi to task and strike afterwards. Shidachi seeks to stifle Uchidachi. Uchidachi takes *wakigamae* to avoid being controlled and the rest is as explained above.

Dai-sanbon (No. 3)

Uchidachi assumes *seigan* and Shidachi takes *gedan hanmi* (*sutemi*) *no kamae* and advance from the right foot. As Shidachi is about to move in (*irimi*), Uchidachi strikes at *shōmen* from *seigan*. Shidachi catches and propels Uchidachi's sword [back] to Uchidachi's right side. Uchidachi immediately responds by striking Shidachi's right *dō*. Shidachi steps forward to the diagonal left from the left foot while simultaneously moving in (*irimi*) and sliding the *kodachi* up so that both swords cross just below the *tsuba*. Shidachi grabs Uchidachi's upper arm and takes two to three paces, then points the *kensen* at Uchidachi's throat. Both resume *seigan*, lower the *kensen* and return to the centre.

Kodachi seigan hanmi (against gedan)

Explanation

This form is also called "*sō no kata*". Shidachi assumes an open stance for Uchidachi to make a strike to *shōmen* (*sutemi*). Shidachi assails Uchidachi with the intention of not dispatching. As explained above, when the upper arm is seized Uchidachi has no choice but to retreat one step to which Shidachi immediately pursues. This is when Uchidachi concedes defeat.

End Notes

1—Probably the single most important event in the nationalisation of traditional swordsmanship and its reinvention into modern kendo was the establishment in 1895 of the Dai-Nippon Butokukai, a private society dedicated to the protection and propagation of Japan's martial culture.

2—With the modifications made to the physical education guidelines for middle schools in 1911 allowing martial arts as elective subjects, the Ministry of Education sponsored an intensive five-week *bujutsu* seminar from November 6 that year at the Tokyo Higher Normal School (Tōkyō Kōtō Shihan Gakkō) to establish procedures and teaching methodology for instruction in schools. Kanō Jigorō (1860–1928) the founder of modern judo and principal of the school, oversaw the first seminar at which the Butokukai's previously formed *kata* were reviewed. It was decided

that the three *kata* created in 1906 were unsuitable for teaching in schools.

3—In October 1912, the committee presented the "Dai-Nippon Teikoku Kendō Kata" (Greater-Japan Imperial Kendo Kata) which consisted of the three *kata* created at the MOE's seminar, plus four more new forms totalling seven *tachi* (long sword) versus *tachi*, and three *tachi* versus *kodachi* (short-sword). Frequent modifications were made to the original version in the ensuing years, but it essentially constituted what modern exponents still practise as the "Nihon Kendo Kata".

4—The three forms previously made by the Butokukai were called *jōdan* (*ten*=heaven), *chūdan* (*chi*=earth), and *gedan* (*jin*=man). Significant opposition was articulated after the *kata* were unveiled. The reasons for resistance were many; due to the hastiness of the *kata* creation (approximately three months from committee inception to the *kata* presentation), there was little chance for debate and in-depth discussion about the content. The main complaints concerned the nomenclature of the fighting stances (*kamae*) used in the *kata*. For example, a *kamae* that resembled *hassō* (sword is held vertically at the right side of the face) in most traditional *ryūha* was formally referred to as *chūdan* (the middle stance in which the sword is typically held out in front of the body).

5—In the Kendo Kata practised today, Uchidachi steps forward with the left foot into *jōdan*.

6—This is a reference to technical progression in traditional arts. For example, comparing to the learning process in calligraphy, initially the student calligrapher must master the basic forms, a stage known as *shin* (真 = essence). When the basic form becomes second nature, that is, an embodiment of the student, individual style can be infused (*gyō* 行 = running style). Following further intensive practice, the student creates a distinctive cursive style which in the final stage is referred to as "grass-writing" (草 = *sō*). This cursive style abbreviates and links the characters resulting in a curvilinear, highly artistic form of writing. The three *kodachi kata* were said to represent this process of mastery.

葉隠

Know your Limits

by Alex Bennett

Hagakure provides a window on life in eighteenth century Japan. We get a sense of the frustrations samurai faced in a time of peace, and the stress that enveloped their existence. Actually, all said and done, they weren't that different to us. They had their foibles, and many of the passages contained in *Hagakure* are surprising in their mundane simplicity.

For example, more than a few vignettes warn the samurai to know his limits and not overindulge when imbibing. The samurai, it seems, had a penchant for getting their fill of rice wine to drown their sorrows—something that many of us can empathize with, I am sure. The urge to temporarily get lost in a bottle, for fun or through the frustration of having to deal with obnoxious people every day, is a fact of life in most cultures around the world.

The repercussions of a night painting the town red nowadays might be an embarrassing photo on Facebook, or a bloodied nose for hitting on somebody you shouldn't have. The stakes for drunken revelry among samurai could be devastating, too. Deadly in fact. At the lower end of the scale, careless drunkenness for a samurai had similar consequences for a young executive or job-seeking graduate caught on an iPhone with his pants down during a temporary lapse of sobriety—a massive black mark on his reputation.

"One should always be careful to behave properly at social gatherings. Careful observation of revelries show that the majority of men are resigned to getting totally drunk. Partaking in alcohol is pleasurable so long as one ceases consumption at an appropriate time. It looks vulgar if one behaves recklessly, and it is an indication of one's character and [low] level of refinement. When drinking, the warrior should be aware that eyes are always upon him. Act appropriately in public." (1-23)

The spectre of alcoholism was also a fact of life, so it seems. "Many men are defeated by alcohol. This is a lamentable fact." As with many things in the precarious lives of the samurai, moderation was the key to keeping one's all-important reputation intact.

"Be attentive to how much you can imbibe without becoming drunk, and do not exceed your limit. Still, one will become intoxicated on occasion. When carousing, be constantly on the alert to deal with any unexpected occurrence…" (1-68)

"Unexpected occurrence" is referring to a brawl, and this could easily escalate into an exchange of cold steel as tempers frayed and testosterone took over. "Drinking is a communal activity, so be very careful of your public appearance." Moderation and knowing your limits—a very pertinent piece of advice even today.

Check out *Hagakure: The Secret Wisdom of the Samurai.*

44th FIK Foreign Kendo Leaders' Summer Seminar Report. Kitamoto City, Saitama Prefecture, Japan. July 21–28, 2017

Steven Hsueh, Southern California Kendo Organization (SCKO), 5-dan
Zia Uddin, Midwest Kendo Federation (MWKF), 5-dan

Introduction

An international cohort consisting of 63 *kenshi* from 45 countries met on July 21, 2017, in Kitamoto City in Saitama prefecture, Japan, to participate in the 44th Foreign Kendo Leaders' Summer Seminar, an event sponsored by the All Japan Kendo Federation (AJKF). The grades of the 52 male and 11 female participants ranged from 3- to 6-dan, with a mix of 52 male and 11 female *kenshi* which included dojo *sensei*, federation officers, as well as current and previous competitors from the World Kendo Championships.

The key objectives of this seminar are to:
1. strengthen practitioners understanding of fundamental kendo principles so that they can become not only better kendo practitioners, but also better instructors in their own federations and dojo

2. develop a deeper understanding and appreciation of kendo and Japanese culture

3. foster friendships and develop bonds in the international kendo community

Opening Day

Day 1 started with all participants meeting at the Kitamoto Gedatsu-kai Centre, which served as the lodging and dining quarters. After checking in and unloading luggage, participants then gathered at the adjacent Gedatsu Renshinkan Dojo to begin the opening ceremony and practice.

Gedatsu Renshinkan Dojo, the training location of the Kitamoto Seminar

This year's Kitamoto seminar was taught by the following instructors:
H8-dan Hamasaki Mitsuru-sensei
H8-dan Kasamura Kōji-sensei
K8-dan Nagao Susumu-sensei
K8-dan Tanaka Hiroaki-sensei

Among the primary instructors were many key teaching staff who assisted in translation, logistics, and supporting instructors and participants during *shidō-geiko* throughout the entire seminar. The following individuals graciously offered their time and assistance:
Matsunaga Masami-sensei (H8-dan), Hayashi Tatsuo-sensei (K8-dan), Ajiro Tadahiro-sensei (H8-dan), Takahashi Tōru-sensei (K8-dan), Satō Yukio-sensei, Nakiri Fuminori-sensei, Miyasaka Masayuki-sensei, Kurose Arinobu-sensei, Alex Bennett-sensei, Katō Junichi-sensei, Okuura Ayako-sensei, Tsurunaga Ryowa-sensei, Kokaze Akira-sensei, Kikawa-sensei, and Otaka-sensei.

The welcome party for all participants and FIK staff and instructors

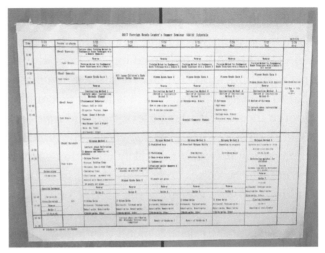

Training schedule

Dorm rooms at the Gedatsu-kai Training Center

The opening ceremony gave the seminar a truly prestigious start, with opening remarks made by several famous instructors and executive members of the Saitama Kendo Federation, AJKF, and the International Kendo Federation (FIK). Among such members in attendance were Yamanaka Shigeki-sensei, president of the Saitama Prefecture Kendo Federation; Takeyasu Yoshimitsu-sensei, former president and honorary advisor to the AJKF; and Fukumoto Shūji-sensei, Vice President of the AJKF. After a commemorative group photo, the opening ceremony then transitioned into *mawari-geiko*, followed by a brief *shidō-geiko* with the instructing staff.

Later in the evening, participants attended a welcome party at the Gedatsu Center which was attended by the mayor of Kitamoto City, Mr. Genouzono Takaaki, who welcomed the trainees to the city. It was the general consensus among the international trainees that they felt truly welcomed and honoured to have this opportunity to learn in Japan from such prestigious instructors and staff members.

Kitamoto Training

The general daily schedule of the Kitamoto seminar included the following:

06:30–07:30: *Bokutō ni yoru kendō kihon waza keiko hō* (*bokutō* basics)
08:00–08:30: Breakfast
08:30–11:30: Nippon Kendō Kata and kendo basics
12:00–12:30: Lunch
13:30–15:30: Instructor's Seminar: *kihon*, *shinpan* training, *waza*, and drills
15:30–16:30: *Shidō-geiko*
18:30: Dinner
20:00: Seminar: *Bōgu* repair, Anti-Doping Lecture
22:30: Lights out

Although not officially on the schedule, there was an "optional" *asa-geiko* which started at 05:30. This was a 30-45 minute open *keiko* which was attended by *sensei* and participants who wished to get additional basics training and *keiko* before the start of the day's agenda. Approximately 15-20 participants took advantage of this session each morning.

Asa-geiko served as an excellent chance to apply all concepts learned during the previous day, as well as another opportunity to spend time working on fundamentals. Here, I practised much of my time with Katō Jun'ichi-sensei, who reminded me to "forget the tricks when going against higher-ranked sensei, and train yourself to go for *men* honestly and in a straightforward fashion". Katō-sensei taught me that in *uchikomi* practice there is much preparation prior to the strike through use of *tame* and *seme*—all to build tension against the *motodachi*. The difficulty of practising *uchikomi* isn't solely repetition—it was the need to be consistently focused and mindful of building tension, executing the correct movement, and retaining correct *zanshin* throughout each strike. If we don't consider these elements thoroughly during and after *keiko*, and just simply go through an entire exercise mindlessly and in a mechanical fashion, it would be difficult to progress and develop oneself in their kendo journey.

All seminar participants were also provided with The Official Guide for Kendo Instruction by the AKJF and The Regulations of Kendo Shiai and Shinpan by the FIK. The seminar focused in depth on the training method for fundamental kendo techniques with a *bokutō* (*Bokutō-ni-yoru kendō kihon-waza keiko-hō*) and the Nippon Kendō Kata. This was led by Hamasaki-sensei, who provided special emphasis on the finer details of these two components in kendo. All Kitamoto participants were required to have had some degree of experience and knowledge in both *kata* and *bokutō* basics. However, it was during the morning sessions where the finer details on distance, *kamae*, timing, and movement were taught.

For the Nippon Kendō Kata, participants were asked to be aware of the difference between *issoku-ittō-no-maai* and *yokote-no-maai*. In *issoku-ittō-no-maai*, the *kenshi* is able to take a single step forward to strike, similar to what is emphasised when training in basic *uchikomi*. It is also utilised throughout most of the forms in *kata*. A distinction, however, is that we must retrain our minds even further regarding the parts of the Japanese katana, not just the *shinai*. For example, the katana has a part called the *yokote*, which is the dividing point between the sword's tip and blade. The distance where the *yokote* of both *kenshi* intersect is called *yokote-no-maai*. We must be aware of this because it is the distance both *kenshi* must finish at the end of all ten *kata*. *Maai*, or distance and

timing, is therefore a critical component that needs to be readily considered when studying the Nippon Kendō Kata.

Additionally, in regard to timing, the relationship between *uchidachi* and *shidachi* during each individual *kata* was also constantly emphasized. The pace and rhythm of each movement is primarily conducted by *uchidachi*, whose role serves as the teacher, whereas *shidachi* is the student. Quite often many people get nervous or impatient when going through all ten *kata*, causing one to attempt to complete each motion quickly in a rushed fashion. It is important to be mindful of the present but without losing concentration throughout. This is one of the important benefits of studying it to become a more complete kendoka.

Proper body mechanics were demonstrated by both Hamasaki-sensei and Tanaka-sensei. Participants were asked to mirror, correct, repeat, and refine numerous times under Hamasaki-sensei's supervision. A common theme was to be readily aware of the back foot when completing each individual *kata*, especially in Ippon-me, where *shidachi* completes the *waza* in *jōdan-no-kamae*. During Ippon-me, many *shidachi* become overly focused on the position of the hands and leave the back foot dragging too far apart from the front foot when assuming *jōdan-no-kamae* at the end of the *waza*. Instead, the feet must still be the correct distance from each other, where the toes of the right foot are aligned with the heel of the left. It seems common sense to have the feet in such a position, but it can be quite easy to forget, especially when one is trying hard to focus during a grading, and even more so when under the constant gaze of 8-dan sensei from Japan!

The technical and cultural components of kendo were taught by Nagao-sensei, who emphasized topics such as the importance of *chakuso*, or the manner of wearing clothing and *bōgu*. The back of the *keikogi* must be straightened so that there are no excess folds or overlaps when it is worn. Additionally, the bottom edge of the *hakama* must be angled slightly downward to the floor instead of parallel, with the front edges of the *hakama* lightly touching the top of the foot. A lot of thought went into the development of *kendogi* and *bōgu*, and the *hakama* itself is no exception. The reason why *hakama* are trouser-like comes from *yabusame* (Japanese horseback archery). The *hakama* was built with inseams in order to be able to manoeuvre on a horse during battle. Additionally, there are six pleats in the *hakama*—five in the front, one at the rear. Each symbolises six important values derived from Confucianism: *jin* (humanity), *gi* (justice), *rei* (courtesy), *chi* (wisdom), *shin* (faithfulness), and *makoto* (sincerity). With such examples, Nagao-sensei taught that budo and culture are seamlessly intertwined, and both need to be regularly studied when one progresses themselves further in the study of kendo.

Nagao-sensei also strongly emphasised the interconnectivity of kendo drills towards *shiai*. When developing a *keiko* program, one must consistently be aware of how the movements in *kihon suburi* connect themselves to *uchikomi*, which then builds on *waza* development, followed by *keiko*, and then ultimately being tested during *shiai*. Rooted in all this is *kihon* development through *suburi*, which therefore must be done correctly and with a strong spirit, otherwise all other subsequent elements cannot build off one another. As a result, Nagao-sensei led participants in an extended session of *suburi* of approximately 500 *shōmen* strikes with full *kiai*. Although word has it that in past seminars participants completed over 1,000 *suburi*, Nagao-sensei strictly emphasised that we perform each of our 500 strikes with complete focus, which itself was exhausting. Indeed, the philosophy was applied even during *kirikaeshi*, where Nagao-sensei asked participants to forget about counting how many strikes are done, but to perform the repeated *sayu-men* strikes until we could barely have one last breath for the final *shōmen* strike. One of Nagao-sensei's key points was that the focus of kendo needed to be on the quality of drill, with special focus on how it connected itself progressively towards *keiko* and *shiai*. A *kenshi* should consider how their *suburi* movement translates towards executing correct *uchikomi*, which then builds towards correct *waza* development, which then is applied through *keiko* and ultimately *shiai*. By creating practices with such a framework in mind, *kenshi* not only constantly

Steve and Zia with Head Instructor H8-dan Hamasaki Mitsuru-sensei

Steve and Zia with co-Head Instructor H8-dan Kasamura Kōji sensei

examine how they are conducted, but place even greater emphasis on the proper development of kendo basics.

The afternoon sessions which were led by Kasamura-sensei focused generally on either *shinpan* training or drills/*waza* development with a focus on how to properly execute *ōji*- and *shikake-waza*. Most, if not all, of the techniques are found in Chapter 7 of The Official Guide for Kendo Instruction and followed The Training Method for Fundamental Kendo Techniques with a Bokuto. Kasamura-sensei emphasised the importance of staying relaxed when practising *waza* because if one's movements are too stiff, one cannot correctly get the timing needed to apply the technique. Moreover, if the body is too rigid it is easy for your opponent to read your intention, and therefore makes it difficult for the *waza* to be effective. This was clear to see when Kasamura-sensei demonstrated *waza* such as *men-suriage-dō*, which require flexibility and correct distance. The point of Kasamura-sensei's instruction was that all combinations and options are possible during *waza* practice, but one needs strong fundamentals and a relaxed body to execute each *waza* sharply and correctly. Only by building strong basics can a *kenshi* begin to more creatively apply techniques appropriate to the situations during *keiko* and *shiai*.

Kasamura-sensei also lectured on the key principles of being a *shinpan* and emphasised the weight of responsibility placed upon *shinpan* during *shiai*,

Children from Gedatsu Renshinkan Dojo practised shiai to help Kitamoto participants in shinpan training. They fought intensely so shinpan had to of course give their best effort.

Bogu craftsman during an evening session to provide repairs and teach us how to fix kendo equipment

regardless of the level. Volunteers were then assigned to practice mock *shiai*, while others practised as *shinpan*.

On one afternoon, young members of the Gedatsu Renshinkan Dojo, whose facility we were using during the seminar, were asked to compete in mock team *shiai* while participants trained as *shinpan*. The sheer speed, energy, and vigour these children had was exceptional, and it required full concentration and effort to make sure one was judging accurately and correctly. On many occasions, Kasamura-sensei and Nagao-sensei would halt matches to evaluate the judgement of the *shinpan*, correct mistakes, and provide additional commentary on improving movement and decisions. This was especially so when serving as *shinpan* for children, because a poor decision not only leaves a bad impression on parents but can also demoralise a young child who is trying their utmost to be victorious.

A full day of instruction would typically close with an hour-long *shidō-geiko* session, during which participants could practise with all the teachers. In the evenings following dinner, participants attended seminars on a range of topics, one such being an interesting lecture on anti-doping by Dr. Miyasaka Masayuki, head of the FIK's anti-doping committee. Dr. Miyasaka explained how banned substances—including steroids, stimulants, and doping agents—created unfair advantages during competition. He also explained the policies behind the World Anti-Doping Agency (WADA) and their implementation in current and future kendo events. In the recent WKC, Dr. Miyasaka spearheaded a pilot project which required the testing of high-level competitors, including the world champion, immediately after winning the individual

*Steve Hsueh learned to repalm his own **kote** from master craftsman Ito Seiichiro*

A sea of young competitors during the opening ceremony of the All Japan Children's Budo Rensei Tournament

Approximately 3,000 children from all over Japan participated in the All Japan Children's Budo Rensei Tournament

event. It was the intention of the FIK to expand this program and include more competitors in future events. Dr. Miyasaka also provided participants with links to monitoring agencies and encouraged coaches to regularly review the list of prohibited substances, which gets updated on at least an annual basis. Considering the increasing skill level of competitors in international kendo, the FIK will be increasing its vigilance through voluntary and mandatory testing in order to prevent issues associated with doping that have unfortunately been prominent in many sports around the world.

Two of the evening sessions included visits from *bōgu* craftsmen who could do simple repairs on attendee's *bōgu*. The visit from these craftsmen was greatly appreciated, as they not only provided repairs free of charge, but at times even gave attendees needle and thread so that they could learn how to stitch and repair armour themselves! Both events were exceptionally insightful because it was an opportunity for participants to see first-hand the amount of work required to construct kendo armour, as well as the ingenuity used by craftsmen to repair wear and tear from regular daily kendo practices.

On Sunday July 23, a special morning session was held in which participants travelled by bus to attend the All Japan Children's Budo Rensei Tournament at the Nippon Budokan in Tokyo, in which over 3,000 young *kenshi* throughout Japan competed in kendo basics and shiai. There was a wonderful ceremony where all 3,000 kendo youths entered the Budokan floor for the opening ceremony, a stunning sight especially because a majority of international

Mealtimes together

Steve Hsueh with Stepan Pavel (Czech Republic) and Chinzo-rig Tugsgerel (Mongolia)

federations consisted of much less than 3,000 adults and children combined.

At least three training sessions a day for a week was no doubt an exhausting for all of the participants. However, it was also a once-in-a-lifetime opportunity to not only train among some of the most respected sensei in the world, but to also train together with *kenshi* who loved and saw the importance of kendo in everyday life. The week ended with a *sayonara* party where each room performed an entertaining skit for all attendees. In the end, the bonds and friendships built were no doubt evident from the smiles and laughter shared with one another through training. The seminar finished with a grading examination for participants. The panel of examiners included famous instructors such as Kakehashi-sensei, Ajiro-sensei, Ujiie-sensei, and Yamanaka-sensei. Many participants successfully passed thanks to the strong emphasis on kendo fundamentals during the seminar. Ultimately all *kenshi* during this exam would leave the seminar with many lessons learned to improve themselves as *kenshi* and leaders for their dojo and federations.

Acknowledgements

The Kitamoto Seminar provided *kenshi* with an even more solid foundation on the many facets of kendo, from the execution of proper technique, to a better understanding of why we perform such specific rituals before, during, and after *keiko*. It's important to note that although training is rigorous, it is not solely intended to build one's ability in *shiai*, although this is an undeniable and important part of kendo. The seminar stresses the development of solid basics through rigorous training. Through these proper basics one improves their performance in *shiai* and allows one to enjoy kendo as a lifetime pursuit in hopes of cultivating a deeper understanding of martial arts.

The US delegates for the 2017 Foreign Kendo Leaders Seminar, Steven Hsueh and Zia Uddin, would like to express our deepest thanks to the instructors who taught us during the seminar. We are also extremely grateful to the staff from both the Gedatsu Renshin-kan Dojo and the All Japan Kendo Federation for planning and coordinating this event in an extremely professional and accommodating fashion. We would like to also thank our federation presidents and the All United States Kendo Federation (AUSKF) for selecting us to represent our nation at this FIK event. We highly recommend this seminar to future kenshi who have a deep dedication to kendo. We also look forward to sharing our experiences and lessons to others, with hopes to promote kendo in our own federations through continued training and guidance.

Advice for Future Participants
Zia Uddin, Kendo 5-dan, Choyokan Kendo Dojo, Midwest Kendo Federation

Begin your own strenuous training before the seminar. While the training was challenging, it was very enjoyable and doable if you are prepared. For example, one afternoon the *sensei* had us do 5+ sets of: 1. *ji-geiko* for about a minute; 2. continuous *kirikaeshi* until the whistle; and 3. continuous *men* strikes until the whistle. Earlier in the morning it was 500 *suburi*. There were several participants that got injured or could not finish practice. Please know your limits, but if you prepare, it will be fine.

The breakdown of the participants was three 6-dan, 13 5-dan, 21 4-dan, and 26 3-dan. The seminar is one in which you get out of it what you put into it, so practise with everyone, especially those better than you. I made it a point to practise with the 6-dan every chance I got. You can partner with other seminar participants throughout the week so do your homework and see who a good partner would be to learn from.

Practise your shinpan skills. The *sensei* constantly commented that the level of refereeing was not good, but that it got better over the week.

If you are bothered by snoring, bring earplugs.

There are Japanese washing machines, but you will have to air dry your *gi* and *hakama*. If you can, bring compression shorts or leggings so your *hakama* is less wet after practice

Examinations results

Room 203 at the end of the ceremony. Front row (l-r): Darryl Tong (New Zealand) and Zia Uddin (USA). Backrow (l-r): Sam Tsai (New Zealand), Kris Inting (Phillipines), Bernard Yehuda (Austrailia), Steve Hsueh (USA), Jason Carvalho (Hawaii), Stephen Hladsky (Canada), and Horacio Vasconcelos (Mexico)

My personal opinion is to practise with the same three or four *sensei* throughout the week rather than trying to practise with each *sensei* once.

Practice getting your *bōgu* on fast, especially during *keiko*. If you do you will be able to practice with three or four *sensei* in each practice.

Watch what you can do for the *sensei*. For example, during meals you can collect their plate. You should make sure your *rei* is at a high level throughout the seminar.

Bring a notepad. There are many things that the *sensei* say slightly differently, and one explanation may not make sense, but after hearing another perspective it may be an "a-ha" moment for you. Also, your roommates may have things on how they teach their students which may be different than what you are learning.

Steven Hsueh, Kendo 5-dan, Butokuden Kendo Dojo, Southern California Kendo Organization

Prepare business cards and gifts for your new friends, including participants, FIK staff, and *sensei*. Some items that were exchanged included dojo/federation *tenugui*, key chains, fridge magnets, and small food or drinks. A small gift goes a long way towards making lasting friendships.

Bring at least three *keiko-gi* and two *hakama*. The summers are hot, and you will be training at least three times a day. Take advantage of break times to dry your *dōgi* as much as possible!

Water and fluids. Never underestimate your need to stay hydrated during training, especially if you have never experienced a Japanese summer. Electrolyte tabs are helpful to prevent cramps and heat exhaustion if you're the type to sweat profusely.

Although it's difficult to get up early in the mornings, go to the 05:30 *asa-geiko*. There is no air-conditioning during these mornings, but you will make the most out of your week to train in *uchikomi* with Katō-sensei and all other *kenshi* who make it to this open *keiko*.

Line up your shoes as neatly as possible along with your roommates. Kendo is a lifestyle where orderliness is just as important as improving oneself through *keiko*.

Talk to and learn from the *sensei* as much as you can. This is a one-week opportunity to train with the best. Although speaking Japanese is very helpful, many of the *sensei* speak very good English and are willing to help you learn and improve.

Don't focus on just training solely with famous 8-dan *sensei* during *shidō-geiko*. *Keiko* is only 30-45 minutes long, and you should make the most of your time practising with as many *sensei* as possible. Other *sensei* can provide just as much critical advice to improve your kendo.

Bring one set of semi-formal attire (light shirt and slacks, no suits needed) to use at the opening ceremony, *sayonara* party, and All Japan Youth Taikai tour. These events have a slightly formal atmosphere, and it's important to represent your federation well and look appropriate for the event.

Bujutsu Jargon Part 11

Reference guide covering various bujutsu-related terminology

Bruce Flanagan MA
Lecturer - Kaichi International University

 # 73
入門
nyūmon

Literally *nyū* means "to enter" and *mon* means "gate/entrance". The term, often used in the verb form *nyūmon-suru* (入門する), means to join a school or commence learning something, usually a traditional art form under the guidance of a teacher (*shi* 師). The character *mon* (門) is found in the words disciple (*montei* 門弟), student (*monkasei* 門下生), pupil (*monjin* 門人), beginner (*nyūmon-sha* 入門者), and a written guide for beginners (*nyūmon-sho* 入門書). Expulsion from a school for breaking its codes of conduct or excommunication from a school is *hamon* (破門).

The troops of renowned Sengoku period military commander Takeda Shingen (1521-1573) carried banners into battle displaying a quote from Sun Tzu's *The Art of War*: "Be swift as the wind, quiet as the forest, fierce as fire, and strong as the mountains." The full quote on the banners read "*Hayaki-koto kaze-no-gotoku, shizuka-naru-koto hayashi-no-gotoku, shinryaku-suru-koto hi-no-gotoku, ugokazaru-koto yama-no-gotoku*" and this has since been abbreviated into the four-character-compound *fū-rin-ka-zan*.

 # 74
風林火山
fū rin ka zan

 # 75
身
mi / shin

This character means "flesh" or the "physical body" and features prominently in *bujutsu* terms. Some examples of the "*mi*" reading are: breakfalls (*ukemi* 受け身); a stance in which the body is positioned diagonally to the line of attack (*hanmi* 半身); stepping or moving in close to an attacker (*irimi* 入り身); strikes and kicks to the body (*atemi* 当て身); and sacrifice moves or disregard for the self (*sutemi* 捨て身). The "*shin*" reading can be seen in the terms: whole body (*zenshin* 全身), upper or lower half of the body (*hanshin* 半身), mind and body (*shinshin* 心身), and the section of a blade which is sheathed or hidden in a scabbard (*tōshin* 刀身).

 # 76

試し
tameshi

Noun form of the verb *tamesu* "to test / to try out". Historically the test cutting of human body parts, corpses, or live victims with a sword was known as *tameshi-giri* (試し斬り). The test cutting of objects such as bundled straw, tatami mats, or bamboo is also called *tameshi-giri* but is written with a different character (試し切り), and the objects themselves are referred to as *tameshi-mono* (試し物). The board-breaking popularised by karate and taekwondo is known as *tameshi-wari* (試し割り) and may include the breaking of roof tiles, slabs of ice, concrete blocks, or baseball bats.

 # 77

奥
oku

Interior or inner workings and, in the martial arts, often alludes to something that is guarded, secret, or that is not intended to be visible or known to outsiders. The most advanced teachings of a martial art and, in some cases, the most guarded or secret techniques are known as *okugi* or *ougi* (奥義). In certain *koryū* schools these techniques may be referred to as *oku-den* (奥伝) or *oku-yurushi* (奥許し). In terms of combat or game strategy, a little-known but formidable technique or hand that is not often used may be called *oku-no-te* (奥の手).

 # 78

伝
den

Means "teaching/transmission". The character is commonly used in *bujutsu*-related terms such as: secret teachings (*hiden* 秘伝), correct transmission (*shōden/seiden* 正伝), direct transmission (*jikiden* 直伝), all teachings (*kaiden* 皆伝), and oral teachings (*kuden* 口伝) that teachers pass directly to their students verbally without making written records. Techniques in certain *koryū* schools are classified as basic-level teachings (*shoden* 初伝), intermediate-level teachings (*chūden* 中伝), and advanced-level teachings (*okuden* 奥伝).

 # 79

月謝
gessha

A monthly tuition fee paid by a student to a teacher or school. Studying or practising an art, sport or skill or taking lessons from a teacher or coach is collectively termed *narai-goto* (習い事). In instances in which fees are not deposited electronically, a cash payment is presented to the teacher once a month often in a special lesson-fee envelope (*gessha-bukuro* 月謝袋). The teacher will later remove the money, stamp their name on the front of the empty envelope, and return it to the student as a record of payments received. The envelope can generally be reused for one financial or academic year.

Bibliography

• *Kōjien* (*Daigohan*), Iwanami Shoten, 2004.
• *Nihon Budō Jiten* (*Zusetsu*), Sasama Y., Kashiwa-Shobō, 2003.

KENDO FOR ADULTS

By Hatano Toshio (Courtesy of *Kendo Nihon*)
Translated by Alex Bennett

Hatano Toshio-sensei was born in January 1945 in Musashi Murayama, Tokyo. After graduating from Kokushikan High School and Nihon University, he became a salaryman for a few years before establishing the Nanbudō Kendōgu shop in 1971. He passed the 8-dan exam on his second attempt in 1994. He serves as an advisor for the West Tokyo Kendo Federation, and is Suruga University Kendo Club Shihan, Musashi Murayama City Kendo Federation president, and leader of the Kinryūkan Dojo.

Part 6: What I Focussed on in Shinsa

I received a letter from a salaryman. He wrote: "After reading your column, I realised the importance of really working hard in the fundamentals of kendo. I have been thinking about restarting kendo after a long break, and decided to only after I had completed a total of 100,000 *suburi*. I finally completed my target the other day after ten months and have started kendo again at a local dojo."

One-hundred-thousand *suburi* in ten months means 10,000 a month, or around 300 a day. He did this every day without a break. This is a wonderful feat, and if I'm honest, I don't know if I could complete it so diligently. If this reader continues kendo in the same vein, then there is no doubt that he will improve in leaps and bounds.

In this instalment, I will discuss a topic that many mature *kenshi* are concerned about. That is,

promotion examinations, or *shinsa*. Allow me to start by introducing my personal experience.

I have not passed every exam on my first attempt. It took me six tries before I managed to pass 6-dan. Still, looking back on it, I believe my five failures contributed greatly to my overall understanding of kendo, and dare I say it, growth as a human being. In the old days we had to sit a preliminary examination conducted by the Tokyo Kendo Federation before we were allowed to attempt the national 6-dan exam. I passed the preliminary test as the youngest candidate. I figured that as I was the youngest, I must be the strongest, and If I don't pass then nobody can.

With that arrogant attitude I took my *kamae* with an air of haughtiness and contempt for my opponents. When the bout commenced, my opponent took me by surprise and attacked me relentlessly. All I could

28

do was dodge his strikes and I didn't land even one valid hit. I put my gear away before the results were even announced. I knew I had failed.

On my second attempt, I was aware of why I failed the first time. I was able to strike my opponent, but I still failed. That is when I really started to analyse what was going wrong and became quite concerned. All my kendo colleagues and *sensei* were convinced that I would pass, so I arrived home to a constant barrage of phone calls. This happened for five attempts.

On my sixth challenge, I thought that I performed very well. Looking back on it, I realised that until then I had never really destabilised my opponent before striking. I must have just been hitting randomly. I finally started to listen to the various pieces of advice from my seniors. My numerous attempts at 6-dan turned out to be quite a humbling experience.

Several years before attempting the 7-dan examination I received instruction from Sekine-sensei, a former policeman in the Tokyo Metropolitan Police Department. After retirement, Sekine-sensei established his own private dojo. He repeatedly told me how determined he was to help me pass the examination on my first attempt. I didn't want to let him down and trained with him as much as I could. After I passed, he told others that "Hatano was training like a man possessed. That is the only way anyone can pass the 7-dan test."

I have a history of passing all odd number grades on my first try. I joked that if they still had 9-dan, then I would get that on my first go. Most of the even number grades took me two attempts or more. In fact, I managed to pass the 8-dan examination on the second attempt.

One shouldn't be concerned how many times it takes to successfully make the grade. Each time I failed, I learned many new things about my kendo, and it provided a platform for further improvement. In fact, failing a few puts you in a good position to pass the next grade relatively smoothly. Notwithstanding, if you fall into the trap of thinking that passing is contingent on how many times you manage to strike your opponent rather than fixing your shortcomings, then even if you finally manage to pass 6-dan after 10 attempts, 7-dan will be further away.

After failing, many people increase the frequency of their training. This is not necessarily a bad thing, but the most important course of action is to learn from your misses and seek to right what you were doing wrong. Otherwise the same thing will just keep happening.

There are always reasons for failing and reasons for passing. The point is to reduce the number of reasons for failure. To this end, it is useful to ask trustworthy kendo colleagues in your midst to give candid feedback. Especially as you get older and your rank gets higher, if you don't ask for somebody's advice they are not likely to offer it to you voluntarily. It is of great consequence when the *sensei* you train with comment on your improvement and that you look set for the big day. When you are ready, the result will take care of itself.

If you have an eye on the future you should avoid becoming too competitive and preoccupied with winning at all costs. Anybody who does kendo will know of the great master Mochida Moriji-sensei and his famous words: "It took me many years before I mastered the fundamentals of kendo." Mochida-sensei didn't practice *kihon* every training. I suspect that he was honing his basics every time he sparred. "That was not a 7-dan level *men* strike. No matter how many times the opponent concedes defeat, I shouldn't be fooled into thinking it was good enough…"

I can only imagine that this was the kind of thing going through his mind each day. Even with such seemingly inconsequential matters of how he grips his *shinai*, I am sure that *kihon*, the fundamentals, was the only thing on his mind when he sparred. After many years of thinking like this, it should come as second nature without the need to think about it anymore. This is what he meant by "It took me many years before I mastered the fundamentals of kendo."

I was competitive in the sense that I wanted to climb my way up the ranks faster than my peers. I concentrated on the little things like my left-hand grip, where my right hand is, *kamae* etc… I discarded my pride and was not concerned about being struck in training. Gradually I was able to fit all the little pieces together, and that was when I finally understood what Mochida-sensei meant.

It is difficult to maintain this mindset all the time. If you make a concerted effort to do it, I think it will have a considerable effect on your progress. Still, when people put their *men* on and take their *shinai* in hand, they tend to engage with the intention of striking the opponent and not being struck.

I also have some lingering doubts when practising with people of 3- or 4-dan level, usually university students. I find that they engage in *keiko* as if it was *shiai*. A few years back I remember Morishima Tateo-sensei saying, "In the old days, 3- and 4-dan practitioners would train with 8- or 9-dan *sensei* as if it were *kakari-geiko*. They weren't trying to compete. That is why they got so strong." Nowadays, people don't seem to care for this kind of approach and regardless of who they are up against, all they worry about is not getting hit.

I wonder what it is that they are trying to achieve in *keiko*. They might be quite gifted in *shiai* but their *keiko* is not "grounded". This is what is meant by the ideogram for "*ji*" in *jigeiko*. Without that grounding, you might get results in the short term, but the future will be bleak. I remember in the old days that even if somebody was not particularly successful in *shiai*, they would be a real handful in *keiko*. I don't come across so many people like that anymore. Right from the outset, the only thing *kendoka* are concerned about now is *shiai*, and more *shiai*.

There is one more thing that I believe people attempting the higher grades of 7- and 8-dan should think about carefully. All the examiners are top-class *sensei* in the world of kendo. I remember when I was getting ready for the 8-dan examination, I saw the examiners and knew of them as formidable competitors in their younger days. They had matured into true masters of our discipline serving as examiners. I thought to myself, what is it that such esteemed kendo masters think of as "good kendo"?

At the time, there was a *kenshi* from the police department who did a straightforward style of kendo, but he was unable to pass. I thought that there was something missing in his kendo. It might be discourteous to say so, but it seemed to me that his style was unappealing, and probably difficult for the examiners to put a tick next to his name… If he had just put a little more "frantic resolve" into his approach, he would surely pass even with exactly the same skill level. Examiners see all sorts of kendo. Even the roughest of diamonds will impress as long as they are doing it with everything they have.

Related to the notion of *kurai* (confidence), people with lower grades are quite happy to listen to advice, but the higher the rank the less likely one is to take other people's observations to heart. Especially around the rank of 7-dan, many people have become established members of society with high up positions in their company or organisation. Any suggestions proffered to them about their kendo will be only partially listened to, or even met with a degree of contempt. "Who do you think you are talking to?" This mentality is lamentable indeed. My point is, you must be prepared to take on good advice no matter where it comes from.

Anyway, back to examinations. The examiners are looking to see if the candidate has reached the appropriate level for the grade being tested. They are not, however, looking for a perfect display. This is the case with 8-dan examinations also. It has been known for people to pass even though they didn't score a valid strike. They were judged as having a strong presence that pushed their opponents back, and then matched them when the opponent felt compelled to attack. Even though a decisive strike didn't connect in the sense that nothing would count as *ippon* in a match, the process was intact and the attack itself is still solid. If *zanshin* is demonstrated properly, this is counted as a plus.

Still, to think that you must "score to pass" will lead to a preoccupation with landing a valid strike. You will often hear talk of "hitting the perfect *kote*" or "requiring one good *men* strike" as if it is something easily achieved. It is not. Of course, successful techniques certainly take you closer to the pass mark, but it is not only *waza* that matters. What is required is the right "vibe" or "gravitas".

What is a fitting "gravitas" for each grade? One's *kamae* and appearance are defining factors. Try and put yourself in the shoes of an examiner and think about how you look. What kind of candidate would leave a good impression? Even if there aren't that many points scored, if the posture, striking, and *kamae* are all good, isn't this worthy of a favourable appraisal? Thinking about such things is vital if you seek improvement.

Solo Practice to Compose your Story

In preparation for my 8-dan examination, I wrote what I call "8-dan Conditions" in several articles and placed them in view when I trained. I was sure to practise what I preached and followed my own advice during *keiko*. I will introduce these in a later article.

When I was preparing for my 8-dan examination, I engaged in "solo practice" which consisted partly of "simulation". In the performing arts of Noh and Kabuki, skilled actors can evoke an appropriate reaction from the audience as soon as they enter the stage. Performing in the arts is called "*engi*", which literally means "rendering of the technique". If the actor cries, the audience senses the despair and becomes sad. For an actor to achieve this requires continual and disciplined training.

A performance of budo is called "*enbu*", or "rendering of *bu*". Like the performing arts, a master of *bu* is able to touch the people watching through continued rehearsals. I thought that I could have the same impact or effect on examiners. With this in mind, I engaged in "solo practices" of 2-minute sessions as I rehearsed my "story". These practices were essentially rehearsals of my artistic performance.

"If my opponent attacks *men*, I will strike *debana-men*." Or, "If all I need to do is show one more successful attack, I am ready to pounce the instant my opponent moves…"

In this way, I imagined various scenarios against a striking-dummy. You can't improve in kendo without a partner. In my mind, my striking-dummy outside in the car port was a training partner as well. Because of this training, I was essentially able to "sit" my 8-dan examination in a sense, two or three years before my first real attempt. I didn't do it every day, but whenever I felt the urge.

In those days, the 8-dan examination was only conducted once a year in May. Of course, regular training and running were also a part of my preparation regime. By the time I sat the test for the first time, it felt like it was my sixth attempt. In other words, I had already sat it virtually five times before, so I already had a very good idea of where I was lacking. It is largely because of this experience that I was able to pass the examination on my second go.

As I was preparing this way, I always imagined the conditions and pressures of the test. For example, let's say that I struck *debana-kote*, in which case a successful *men* strike would be a massive boost to my chances. I would imagine this kind of situation, and urged my striking-dummy to "come on, come on…" and hit it the instant it "moved". The idea being that even if the strike was not perfect, the mindset of pro-actively pushing my opponent and coercing him to strike would be readily sensed and appreciated by my "audience".

There are many times when the lack of a "story" is evident. For example, let us assume that an examinee scores a beautiful *men* strike from the outset. If s/he follows up with several unsuccessful strikes thereafter, the examiners are likely to think that the first one was nothing more than a fluke.

This is the result of not having a "story" and losing the plot right at the start. When this happens, two minutes is a long time to fluff your lines. One of the causes of this is the feeling that you must keep striking no matter what. This will work against you.

Also, what about if you score a point. Does that mean as long as your opponent does not strike then they will be unable to pass? Persistently apply pressure focussing on the opponent's *debana*. Your opponent will come forward because s/he feels the pressure to get one back. Even if you are unsuccessful in landing that perfect *debana-men*, the examiners will look up on your performance favourably seeing that you are always taking the initiative rather than defending or hitting randomly.

If you believe that being struck means failure, then you will become depressed and dejected. Just because you get struck doesn't mean that your pay will be docked or that you will be fired from work. That being the case, why is it that so many people get disheartened if they get hit? Why can't they suck it up and go forward positively, fighting fair and square without concern for being struck? People who achieve this mindset will shine in examinations. When you get struck, it is important to control the sense of frustration. This emotional control is called "*kokkishin*", or the "spirit of self-denial". In other words, discipline.

I always create a theme for each training session. When training has finished, I reflect on whether I able to successfully achieve what I set out to do. Success = victory. It doesn't matter whether you get struck in the process or not; the point is to realise the day's training goal. That is where true victory in training lays.

REI

DAN

THE GREATER MEANING OF

KENDO

JI

CHI

VARIOUS SHIKAKE-WAZA

By Prof. Ōya Minoru (Kendo Kyōshi 7-dan)
International Budo University

Translated by Alex Bennett

Ōji-waza techniques are executed as an extension of receiving the opponent's *shikake-waza*, and include *nuki-waza, suriage-waza, kaeshi-waza, uchiotoshi-waza* and so on. This article will focus on *nuki-waza*, but the following points should be kept in mind when executing any *ōji-waza*:

① Do not just respond to your opponent's movement. Always seek to take the initiative (*sen*).

② Carefully discern the kind of *waza* your opponent is attempting, and the timing.

③ Take care to maintain correct distance and move accordingly.

④ Ensure that the blade direction is precise, and the action of receiving and striking is seamless.

⑤ Keep your wrists flexible, and do not block the opponents attack forcefully.

⑥ Receive with the *shinogi* section of the *shinai*.

1. Body and Shinai Movement

Ōji-waza can be executed while moving in various directions as listed below:

① Crossing paths while you go forward

② Moving back

③ Moving forward to the diagonal right

④ Moving forward to the diagonal left

⑤ Moving back to the diagonal right

⑥ Moving back to the diagonal left

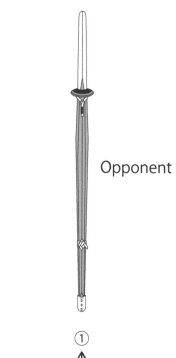

Opponent

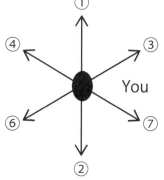

You

32

The *shinai* must be manipulated as you move. Be sure to face your opponent directly the moment you strike otherwise the technique will be too weak to be valid.

With regards to *shinai* manipulation when executing *ōji-waza*:

① *Nuki-waza*→ Avoid contact with the opponent's *shinai* as they attack, and follow up immediately with a counter-technique when they miss the target

② *Suriage-waza*→ Striking on the same side as the opponent's *shinai* is deflected

③ *Kaeshi-waza*→ Striking on the opposite side of the *shinai* immediately after receiving the opponent's attack

④ *Uchiotoshi-waza*→ Striking the opponent's *shinai* down with the blade as they attack

---

2. Nuki-waza
Avoiding the Strike

(a) Avoid by controlling the *maai*

(b) Avoid by changing direction

(c) Avoid by timing

In response to your opponent's *kote* attack, stay where you are as you lift your *shinai* overhead. Just as their *shinai* comes down for the strike to *kote*, your hands will be moving up so it will just miss the target. The shaded area in the illustration represents the "danger zone" for the opponent's *shinai* to hit *kote*. The opponent's *monouchi* and your right *kote* must not come into contact. The top intersection represents a successful *nuki*. Furthermore, depending on the situation, your opponent's attacking speed, and the distance you may combine this motion with (a) and (b) simultaneously.

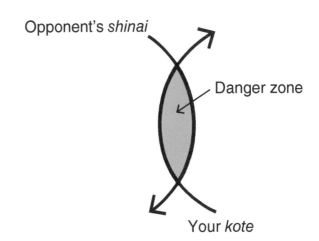

If you prepare to do *nuki-waza* too early, your intentions will become known to your opponent and you will leave yourself open as a result. Similarly, if you leave it too late you will get hit before you move. This is why it is important to pay close attention to your opponent's movement. Ideally, you should strike just as the opponent's failed technique is coming to its conclusion. If you are attempting *nuki* by changing direction you should strike as you move.

[*Nuki-waza* against *men*]

Men-nuki	*Shōmen* (moving back)	
	Hidari-men (move to the right)	
	Migi-men (move to the left)	
	Migi-dō (move forward to the diagonal right)	
	Hidari-dō (move to the left)	
	Kote (move to the left)	

① ***Men-nuki-men*** (Moving back)

Step back from the left foot to avoid the attack to *men* and immediately step forward to counter-strike *men*.

② ***Men-nuki migi-dō*** (Move forward to the diagonal right)

Step forward from the right foot to the diagonal right and strike *dō* as the opponent extends his/her arms. Snap your left foot up as you strike *dō*.

[*Nuki-waza* against *kote*]

Kote-nuki	*Men* (stay where you are and lift your arms up)	
	Men (move back)	
	Kote (lower your *shinai*)	
	Migi-men (move to the left and strike *migi-men* with one hand)	

① ***Kote-nuki-men*** (Stay where you are and lift your arms up)

As your opponent executes an attack to *kote*, stay put and lift your hands overhead so that their *shinai* just misses your *kote*. Immediately strike *men*.

② ***Kote-nuki-men*** (Move back)

As your opponent attempts to strike *kote*, step back from the left foot as you lift your *shinai* overhead, and immediately step in to strike *men* as they miss the target.

Important Points

① With *men-nuki-dō* it is important to have the feeling that you are going to attack *dō* off the mark rather than waiting for the opponent to start their attack to *men* first.

② If you move diagonally forward to avoid the *men* attack be sure to strike while facing the opponent to enable correct blade angle.

③ With *kote-nuki-kote*, the swing as you strike is going to be very small, so compensate for this with a powerful stamp as you hit the target.

I will analyse *suriage-waza* in the next article.

shugyō (n.)

The process of rigorously training and polishing one's mind and body. See *musha-shugyō*.

(AJKF, *Japanese-English Dictionary of Kendo*)

The Shugyō Mind: Part 4   By Alex Bennett

"People who don't look after their equipment will never get good…"

To excel in kendo simply means getting to the dojo as much as possible and training hard, right? Of course, training hard (and smart) is a prerequisite to success. But, as the strongest kenshi will tell you, attention to seemingly insignificant details - like taking good care of your equipment - is just as important.

Six-time All Japan champion, Miyazaki Masahiro, devotes a whole section in his book *Kachi-tsuzukeru Gijutsu* ("Skills to Keep Winning", Sunmark Books, 2017) to this topic: "If you look after your gear, your gear will look after you and help you win…"

Equipment that is not maintained properly is dangerous and may result in injury to you or your opponent. It is not just a matter of checking your *shinai* for splinters, but it is to treat each piece of your *bōgu* with the utmost respect and affection.

Your equipment is worn to protect you in training and competition, so it stands to reason that extra time be taken to look after it properly. For example, if it's a nice day, give your *men* a little time in the sun. Always rub your *men* and *kote* down after training, removing all the sweat and massaging out the *tenouchi* leather.

I know of some people who even wipe their *shinai* with their sweat-soaked *tenugui* after training as if they were cleaning a prized katana. The thin layer of sweat transferred to the bamboo is, to them, like the thin layer of oil applied to a naked blade to stop it from rusting. I know of others who fold their *hakama* meticulously after each *keiko*. A common tendency is not exactly stuffing it in your bag like you would with a sweaty t-shirt and gym shorts, but to roll it up hastily or just hang it up to get to the second dojo faster.

In watching people who take the time to do it properly one senses a feeling of pride in them. You can tell that they are deep in thought reflecting on the day's training. The act is essentially post-*keiko zanshin*, and their *hakama* is as sharp as the day they bought it when they put it on next time.

You may also come across some sensei who refuse to let you fold their *hakama* or pack up their *bōgu* after training. Of course, this is the polite thing to do for a visiting sensei, but if they turn your offer down, the chances are it is because they have their own method and see this is an integral part of their *shugyō*.

Miyazaki-sensei even goes so far as to thank his equipment. "Before and after *shiai*, irrespective of whether I win or lose, I always say a few words to my *bōgu*. 'Thank you. It's because of you that I wasn't hit.' 'Help me out again next time.'… If anybody was around to hear they'd no doubt think it very strange. But, I started getting stronger in kendo after I started to care for my equipment."

We often talk of kendo as being a vehicle for self-development and nurturing respect. Ideally, this is not only directed to the people you train with or those who teach you. The environment where one trains, and the equipment that one uses are just as deserving of veneration.

In an era when *bōgu* is comparatively cheap and easy to replace, this crucial element of kendo *shugyō* is increasingly forsaken. So, why not say a big thank you to your *bōgu* next time you put it on?

THE STATE OF THE JAPANESE KENDOGU INDUSTRY

By Kusanagi Hiroki
Photos: Natalie Rachel Photography,
Montreal, Canada

Recently, we are told, the number of people doing kendo world-wide is increasing. Indeed, 56 countries participated at the 17th World Kendo Championships in 2018—this was three times as many as the inaugural WKC in 1970. This is an encouraging trend when we consider the rapidly aging population in Japan and anecdotal observations that there is a steady decrease in kendo participation in Japan overall.

So what are the implications of these developments in terms of Japan's *bōgu* industry? While it is not surprising that there is still a significant number of *bōgu* retailers throughout Japan, there has been a noticeable surge in internet-based *bōgu* shops directed at the international market.

In Japan, there are only a few *bōgu* shops in each of the 47 prefectures, but more are found in the larger regions. But this is still a substantially greater number than anywhere else in the world. Naturally, then, the majority of the international kendo community who are based outside of Japan would rely on internet vendors in order to meet their kendo equipment needs - a simple case of supply and demand.

In a country where there is no shortage of availability, the price of *bōgu* has been driven down remarkably in recent years. As with products in many industries, the primary reason for this is the availability of cheap labour and outsourcing. Additionally, however, the swell in internet-based suppliers and an increasingly fierce price war between Japanese retailers may also be contributing to the drop in price. What is more, with many locally-based shops aligning with an internet supplier, or creating their own online store, I believe we are witnessing a move towards sustainable business for a number of under-performing local stores around Japan.

Regrettably, however, this has not translated into an increase in the number of Japanese *kendōgu* craftsmen. For the reasons related to the price wars and outsourcing mentioned above, there is in fact a worrying decline in the number of trained people in the workforce in this area. The result is a decrease in the number of genuine Japanese-made sets of *kendōgu* produced and sold.

Perhaps most interesting for the reader is that the skill level of the off-shore workforce has made some noticeable improvement of late. As such, I predict a further and steady drop in the number of Japanese people willing to dedicate their lives to the art of *kendōgu* craftsmanship, conceivably perpetuated by the hesitance of young people to sit in one spot, from morning to evening, with needle and thread in hand. Indeed, I would hazard a guess that shifts in the attitude and aspirations of young people globally will have an impact on the workforce of many handcraft industries.

While this may not be the only reason for the decline in willing and ready apprentices in the *kendōgu/bōgu* manufacturing industry, the fact of the matter is that replacing the skill of a steadily retiring workforce has become a struggle.

Through my work in this business, I am currently left wondering how many Japanese *bōgu* shops actually have the available talent to make or repair an item of kendo equipment? I would estimate that only half have the ability provide a basic repair service.

The reality is that many Japanese kendo practitioners have not actually seen the *kendōgu* repair process, something that would arguably be most interesting to many non-Japanese practitioners. Rather, it appears that it is a more common practice for people to purchase a cheap set of gear and simply dispose of it when it begins to fall apart.

I would also argue that the responsibility for this drop in skilled Japanese *kendōgu* craftsmen falls squarely with the Japanese kendo community for the reasons I have outlined. While we need to explore what steps are required to increase our workforce, I believe that figuring out how to maintain the current numbers, or at the very least slow the decline, is a priority. And there are no easy solutions.

This decline in talent and skill within Japan has indeed put pressure on my own day-to-day work. The lack of available staff has meant that we, too , are forced to out source some of our manufacturing

tasks (although we are committed to keeping the production and repair of our *kote* in-house). However, we must persevere in our attempts to safeguard the future of the craft and continue to train our apprentices.

The work we can produce may be limited by the decline. However, our primary objective is to have as many kendo practitioners as possible witness and learn about the *bōgu* production process and contribute to closing the gap between the craftsperson and the practitioner. This, I believe, will help to build appreciation for the craft, whilst ensuring that the needs of the consumer are also closely monitored. These are important ingredients in strengthening the industry and moving forward.

In meeting the needs of our customers and promoting the long-term use of kendo equipment, it is critical for us, as craftspeople, to make *bōgu* that fits correctly, that is comfortable, and that is easy to use. These two goals—nurturing a rapport between craftsman and practitioner, and developing innovative and comfortable gear—should be foremost in any *kendōgu* craftsman's mind.

To drive the point home, I strongly encourage the reader to take advantage of any opportunity to observe a *kendōgu* craftsman in action. I am confident that watching a craftsman at work will demonstrate the level of skill involved, and help to nurture appreciation for the value of handcrafted *bōgu*.

Previously I mentioned that the level of needlework skill was improving in the outsourced workforce. Nevertheless, it is my observation that there is still a vast number of these men and women who do not actually do kendo, and many more who have not even seen it. Surely this lack of kendo experience in the craftsman would be cause for concern as it is unreasonable to expect a non-practitioner to truly appreciate the needs of a diligent practitioner. Indeed, this is seldom the case with Japanese *kendōgu* craftsmen as it is a love for kendo that leads them toward a career in the industry.

This is particularly true when it comes to fashioning a pair of *kote*. Even if the ideal cut and pattern are provided to the craftsperson, the inability of the needle-bearing non-practitioner to make small adjustments is very noticeable in the finished product. If they do not have experience in holding and manipulating a *shinai*, how could we expect anything more? When it comes to breaking in a pair of *kote*, the quicker the better. So if a pair of *kote* are not sewn to complement the grip on the *shinai*, more strain is placed on the leather as it adjusts; this leads sooner to rips and tears as well as all-round decreased durability. Arguably, only a practicing kendoka would truly understand the adjustments needed to any pattern to enhance the initial fit of the glove.

When the *tenouchi* leather on a set of *kote* (which have been made with a working knowledge of kendo) requires replacement, it is the replacement process that can and should enhance the overall usability of the gauntlets. This is due to the fact that, with training, the shape of the glove and deer hair has moulded to the user's hand. As such, the kendoka craftsperson will be able to use this information to better fashion the *tenouchi* leather to the natural shape of the customer's hand.

With some simple research, one can discern what to look for in a set of kendo equipment, distinguish what equipment has been made by a practising kendoka, and determine what "quality" feels like. I encourage the reader to try on different "levels" of *bōgu*, and I am confident that, through this investigation, a clear picture of the differences will emerge.

And with a similar mind-set, if you find yourself in the market for new *bōgu*, I would recommend asking the supplier if their service can offer an on-site craftsperson who not only practises kendo, but who can also provide a repair service. Aside from the reasons I have outlined here related to practical kendo knowledge of the craftsperson, unavailability of an in-house repair service is likely to cost more money in the long run, whether this be because of costs associated with outsourcing and shipping, or having to buy a completely new pair of kote once the initial pair wears out.

Ultimately, my primary concern is that entering the marketplace with the above points in mind increases the likelihood that the skill of Japanese kendo craftspeople is kept alive. This is in the best interests of every kendo practitioner. While I have a vested interest in this as a *bōgu*-maker, the survival of the craft itself is much more important from my perspective.

Now, the reader may reason that such information could be garnered from any *kote* with time. However, as mentioned above, the longer it takes for *kote* to be broken in, the more prone it is to damage. Consequently, repairs will potentially include the use of extra materials to sew up a number of rips and tears formed during that process, and the glove will, once again, need to be broken in.

The more material needed in the repair, the bulkier the glove becomes. The glove is therefore stiffer and less durable, with the ongoing price of repair an unnecessary expense. This is the unfortunate life-cycle of kendo equipment that is produced through an outsourcing approach by a non-practitioner craftsperson behind the needle and thread.

By all means, shop around. But I encourage you to consider all of the above before making a decision about your purchase based solely on the price tag. Indeed, purchasing equipment from a supplier without the ability to make and repair their own goods should be a consideration for those committed to improving their kendo and keeping themselves, and others, safe. *Bōgu* will always require repairing at some stage, but it should never be considered a disposable item.

As a craftsperson, I am committed to making *kote* that stand the tests of time and training. This is my contribution to kendo, and it is what drives me to do it every day. The craftsperson's skill may only be one piece of the pie, but it is still important to the future of kendo in my opinion.

BUYING YOUR FIRST SET OF
KENDŌ-GU?

ALEX BENNETT

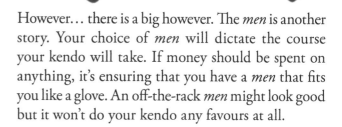

You've been to the local dojo for a look. You liked what you saw. Throngs of frenzied jedi duelling with bamboo sabres. Could this be the martial art that will change your life? There is only one way to find out. You join the local dojo.

Progress in kendo is typically not that fast. It takes a long time to get used to the Japanese words, master the awkward fighting stance, and swing the *shinai* in unison with "body and spirit." Depending on the dojo, the first few months will be spent learning footwork and *suburi*. Gradually you will move on to striking practice, and then the moment of truth. *Kendō-gu* time!

This is exciting and daunting at the same time. Apart from the fact that you will be entering the merciless world of hit-or-be-hit, purchasing your first set of armour is a big financial investment, especially as you still don't know that much about kendo. You might just find out later on that it is not for you after all.

With this possibility in the back of the mind, the beginner tends to opt for the cheapest set of armour available. There are numerous retailers online who compete to offer ridiculously low-priced sets. Compared to when I first started kendo, the cost of a full set of gear has gone through the floor. You don't have to look very far to find deals as low as $250 a set. On the surface, the gear looks perfectly good. As long as it soaks up the sting of the *shinai* it'll be okay, right? Why pay $2500 when $250 will get you a functional set of armour?

It's true that the market flood of cheap *bōgu* has made kendo accessible to more people. For somebody starting out a cheap set is a logical choice. A beginner doesn't need a pristine lacquered bamboo *dō*, or exquisite hand-stitched *kote* and *tare*. Cheap is fine.

However… there is a big however. The *men* is another story. Your choice of *men* will dictate the course your kendo will take. If money should be spent on anything, it's ensuring that you have a *men* that fits you like a glove. An off-the-rack *men* might look good but it won't do your kendo any favours at all.

There is a very practical reason for this. Around half way down the protective metal grill is a section in which the bars are slightly further apart than the rest. This is called the *mono-mi*, and should be exactly the same level as your eyes. This will give you an undisturbed view of your opponent. If it is too high or low, even by a few millimetres, you will unconsciously crook your head to compensate. This means that your *kamae* will be slightly stilted. This then leads on to flawed technique, muscle pain, and even a higher risk of injury. It will be very uncomfortable and unnatural, but you won't know this because it's your first. Furthermore, even if a cheap *men* does fit well and the *mono-mi* is in the right place, there is a high chance that poor craftsmanship will result in movement of the inner face brace (*uchiwa*). This will cause the *men* to move out of position through use.

So, when you buy your first set of armour, don't worry so much about the *do, tare,* or *kote*. Cheap will suffice. But certainly splash out on a decent *men* tailored to your measurements. Get it made to fit. It'll be your new best friend and will make the kendo experience so much better.

The UTS Kendo Seminar and Open Shield Competition

with H8-dan **Kamei Tōru-sensei** *and H8-dan* **Furukawa Kazuo-sensei**

By Clement Guo

On January 26-29, the UTS Kendo Club hosted the UTS Kendo Seminar and Open Shield Competition, at the University of Technology Sydney in Sydney, Australia. The event featured a three-day seminar followed by the annual UTS Open Shield Kendo Competition on the fourth and final day. This year, the event organisers invited Hanshi 8-dan teachers, Kamei Tōru-sensei and Furukawa Kazuo-sensei from Kumamoto and Hokkaido respectively, to lead the seminar. Both sensei are highly regarded kendo professionals, with significant experience in both competition and coaching. Despite both sensei being 62, they train regularly, compete at the All Japan 8-dan Invitational Kendo Championships (Furukawa Sensei was the 2015 champion), and have active coaching roles with the Japanese national kendo team.

It was a rare opportunity to have such high-level kendo teachers travel to Australia, and over 90 participants from Australia and New Zealand attended this

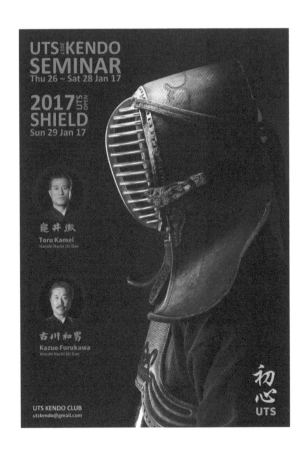

event. The seminar covered a broad range of kendo techniques, from *kihon* (basics) and *waza* (techniques), through to *shiai* and *shinpan* (referee) practice, while the UTS Open Shield provided an opportunity to apply the sensei instruction into practice.

During the *kihon* session, we practised the basics of *men*, *kote*, and *dō* as well as *kirikaeshi*. This began first with *suburi* before wearing *bōgu* in order to ensure that we had correct posture and form. Key focus points from Furukawa-sensei included having big, one-movement cuts (as opposed to pausing at the top), fast but correct *suriashi* (footwork), and maintaining a flow when making multiple cuts. During the *waza* session, we worked on a series of *ni-dan* and *san-dan waza*, like *kote-men* and *kote-men-dō*. We then moved on to practising *shikake-waza* such as *harai-men*, and *ōji-waza* like *men-kaeshi-dō*. During the *waza* exercises we were reminded to apply what we had covered in the *kihon* session to this practice, as well as now adding the *motodachi* (receiver) into the mix and ensuring that each pair maintained a good *maai* (distance), connection, and *seme*.

Instructors

In the later sessions, Kamei-sensei led us through a few mock *shiai* to practise *shinpan* skills during which each *shinpan*'s decisions were scrutinised against the criteria for *ippon*. It was a great opportunity for those who do not often get a chance to act as *shinpan* to try their hand at refereeing a match. Some of the useful feedback was to always be able to see the other *shinpan* in order to be aware of their movements and decisions (rather than focussing only on the competitors), and to move fluidly as a unit around the *shiai-jō*. This is to ensure that each *shinpan* has the best angle to judge the strikes that are made.

Finally, there were two tournaments, which included the UTS Open Shield Competition on the fourth and final day. These tournaments were *ippon-shōbu* with unlimited time, which not only provided a real test of a competitors' ability to score the winning *ippon*, but also challenged the *shinpan* to make the right decisions.

I would like to share three insights gleaned from the event.

Kihon is key to kendo performance

A common message and an undeniable truth is that *kihon* shapes our kendo performance. During the seminar, Furukawa-sensei emphasised the importance of being able to cut *men*, *kote*, or *dō* in a strong, correct, and purposeful manner. Without this, we cannot move onto different and more complex *waza*, all of which require a strong foundation. A habit that was noticed among the participants was a tendency to take a small step forward with the left foot before striking. Furukawa-sensei explained that this defeated the purpose of setting *issoku-ittō-no-maai* and showed a lack of understanding of cutting distance. If we do not correct for this, we will always find ourselves half a step behind the opponent's cuts in a *shiai*. This example was a good reminder to always focus on building correct *kihon* during normal training, so as to set the stage for the development of *waza* and *shiai* performance.

Motodachi is crucial to kendo development

The *motodachi* plays a very important role for the *kakarite* (attacker) and their kendo development.

Kamei-sensei explained it is very easy to take a relaxed approach as *motodachi*, simply opening up for the strike. However, this does not encourage or create the ideal learning environment for the *kakarite* to grasp the pressure, timing and execution of a cut. In the end, both the *motodachi* and *kakarite* will struggle to translate this training to the *shiai-jō*. The correct way to be a *motodachi* is to keep pressure on the *kakarite*. Even when you open yourself for a cut, it should be very slight and only at the last second away from the centre, thereby giving the *kakarite* the feeling of taking the centreline when they attack. After receiving the cut, the *motodachi* should turn sharply and push in with *seme*, creating tension with the *kakarite* as they turn and ready themselves for the next strike. This creates the necessary environment to enable your kendo to perform during the high intensity of *shiai*.

Shiai is the real test of your kendo skills

Shiai provides a real and meaningful test of your kendo skill and ability to score the winning *ippon*. During the event, the *shiai* were all knockouts (no league rounds) and *ippon-shōbu* with unlimited time, so in effect, each *shiai* was a sudden death match from the start. In a way, this format removed all the comfort of a having a 'second chance' in a match, whether as an *ippon* to tie and then win, or having another bout in the pool to overturn an earlier loss. As a competitor, this may seem rather daunting knowing that you could exit for a brief lapse of concentration, a lucky hit, or even a bad *shinpan* call. However, what this produced was a real test of skill for the competitor (and for the *shinpan* too!). Each movement and cut you make must be with purpose and in order to win consistently, you need to rely more on *seme*, wits, and skill to defeat your opponent, rather than power or luck. Personally, I found the UTS Open Shield competition to be more challenging, but also a great way to test my abilities. Suddenly, everything about having good *kihon* and training for *shiai* becomes crucial to success. Applying this mindset going forward, I hope to view each of my *shiai* matches as a way to measure how well I have applied my kendo training into *shiai* performance.

Overall, the event proved to be very insightful; the three points discussed above have given me plenty to try in my regular training. It has also given me a deep sense of admiration for Kamei-sensei and Furukawa-sensei, how they train, and what it takes for them to win. You only need to look at their incredibly successful track record to see where it has taken them.

Magyar-Japan Kendo Club

Name of Club: Hungarian-Japanese Kendo Club (Magyar-Japan Kendo Klub—MJKK)

Year Established: 2000

Club Motto: "破" (*Ha*—to break) and "稽古修練は死ぬまで一生である" (*Keiko shūren wa shinu made isshō de aru*—Practise your whole life, until you die)

Venue: Varosliget Hungarian-English Bilingual Primary School, 1146 Budapest, Hermina ut 9

Number of Members: 80

Classes on Offer: Kendo for adults and children, iaido

Weekly Practice Times:

   Monday: kendo 5:00–6:30pm (children)
                   7:00–8:30pm (adults)
   Tuesday: iaido 7:00–8:30pm
   Wednesday: kendo (children) 5:00–6:30pm
   Thursday: kendo (adults) 7:00–8:30pm
   Friday: iaido 7:00–8:30pm

Instructors: Abe Tetsushi (kendo K7-dan),
             Hunor Mihalik (iaido R7-dan, kendo R6-dan)

What does a typical training session consist of?

After a thorough warm-up we do basic footwork and *suburi* together. Next, beginners and *bōgu* wearers practise separately. Sandor Lapossy teaches beginners, and is doing a great job in helping new members reach *bōgu* level. On Mondays we focus more on basics; Thursdays there is more time for *ji-geiko*.

Club Social Media:

www.mjkk.hu facebook.com/mjkkdojo

Club History:

The head instructor of MJKK is K7-dan Abe Tetsushi-sensei. He received his degree from the International Budo University in Katsuura, Japan. After that, he entered the University of Tsukuba where he has received his master's degree in budo history and philosophy. Between 1992 and 1995 he took part in the JOCV (Japanese Overseas Cooperation Volunteer) program and worked as kendo instructor for the Hungarian Kendo Federation. In 1995, he came back to Hungary, where he still lives. Since 1994 he has been working as a college teacher and technical director of the HKF, and also teaches at the Hungarian-Japanese Kendo Club.

The MJKK iaido group

According to Abe-sensei, he established the MJKK in 2000 because "…as a guest instructor, you don't take full responsibility. You may help the students well but it is not possible to establish a relationship based on mutual responsibility. I wanted my own club where I could follow my own ideas; where kendo was taught with a Japanese approach in a traditional way, not as a competitive sport. Nevertheless, students would enjoy training and improve their lives through the experiences of practising kendo."

Kendo started in Hungary in 1982 and has been going from strength to strength ever since. The Hungarian Men's Team finished third at the World Kendo Championships in both 2012 and 2015.

The Hungarian-Japanese Kendo Club is one of Hungary's major kendo clubs. In Budapest there are three other clubs—Budapest Fönix, Happu Fudo, Aka Tonbo—, but MJKK is one of the biggest with around 80 members. There also has been an iaido class since MJKK's inception where we are proud to have as head instructor the youngest European iaido R7-dan: Hunor Mihalik, a direct student of the late Iwata Norikazu Hanshi. In the kendo class there are four 6-dan teachers (Hunor Mihalik, Aranka Sipos, Yamaji Masanori, and Sakai Yasunori). Many 5-dan kendoka from other clubs also regularly attend our club on a regular basis.

In 2008, a children's kendo class was started to educate a new generation of kendoka who could acquire the basics at a young age. The instructors of the children's kendo group called "Team 破" ("Team Ha", "*ha*" meaning "to break"), Abel Varadi and Marina Boviz, members of the Hungarian National Team, have managed to establish a long-standing and strong team with a friendly atmosphere during the past nine years.

Members of MJKK have also established two new clubs: the Ippon Kendo Club, founded by Tamas Györy and Niki Balazs; and a subsidiary dojo by Robert Nagy and Gyula Morvay. MJKK is also the cradle of such original work as the beautiful leather *tsuba* of Miklos Trum's "Keiko Studio" or Akos Vachter's "Kendo Duel" playing cards.

During its 17-year history, MJKK's training venue has changed three or four time for various reasons, but the club has already outgrown its current dojo. Friendships and relationships have been born here, and I believe, in accordance with the original purpose of its founder, many of MJKK's members and friends have been able to enrich our lives during their time in the club.

Abe-sensei's most important objective is to lead the club in such way that it remains active for 50 or even 100 years, because then it would really mean the successful transmission of kendo culture from Japan.

さらに参ぜよ三十年

"Sara ni sanze yo sanjū-nen"

"Do it again, another thirty years."

Thirty years was the traditional time period for ascetic study. Once that's finished, however, you have to start again. There is no end. Must.

Tsuji Gettan (1648–1727) was a famous swordsman who founded the of Mugai-ryū school of *kenjutsu* in 1695.

Born in the village of Masugimura located in what is now Shiga prefecture, the young Gettan was sent to nearby Kyoto to study under Yamaguchi Bokushinsai. He was only 13 when he started learning swordsmanship from his master, but his diligence and natural ability led to him eventually receiving a licence in the Yamaguchi-ryū. He then departed on a journey to test his mettle against other swordsmen and the elements as many of his contemporaries were wont to do.

Spending most of his time in the mountains around Kyoto, he experienced a number of epiphanies into the deepest secrets in swordsmanship while tempering is body and mind in the ragged mountains. His focus was very much on channelling *ki* through his sword. It was said that the tip of his sword used to look like it was "growing in size" when he faced off against his opponents. Lewd innuendos aside, this observation essentially means that his *ki* and sword were merged into one, thereby giving his weapon a life of its own.

After this sojourn in the mountains he decided it was time to make a living through teaching his art. To this end, Gettan made his way to Edo. But was a completely unknown warrior among many challengers already there. One day when he was strolling down

By
ALEX BENNETT
Based on the book
"KENSHI NO MEIGON" (1998)
by the late Tobe Shinjūrō
Used with author's permission.

a bustling street, a group of samurai decided to hassle him due to his rather odd appearance and demeanour. "Oi bollocks! You lookin' for trouble then?!" Gettan removed his hat revealing an unkempt head of hair and a seriously crazed look in his eyes. He looked like a mountain devil and scared the bejeezus out of his would-be assailants. There was certainly something different about Gettan.

He set up a dojo in the Kojimachi district of Tokyo in 1680, but to his dismay, no warriors showed an interest in learning from him. After all, few people had ever heard of Yamaguchi-ryū. He continued to train on his own all the same, and intensified his efforts in the study of Zen Buddhism. It was the Zen influence that took him to the next stage, and is why he adopted the name "Mugai" from a Zen poem:

"There is nothing other than the One True Way
As vast as Heaven and Earth may be, only the
Way can create this single Righteous Virtue
The One True Way dwells in our hairs, and its
sharpness can slice a fluttering feather in two
And the purest light radiates whenever it manifests"

"Mugai" is written with the kanji 無外, which means

"Nothing other than…" The treatises he wrote pertaining to his style of swordsmanship, such as *Mugai Shinden Kenpō Ketsu* were heavily influenced by Zen teachings, and later disciples of the tradition started calling his swordsmanship the Mugai-ryū.

His fame began to spread, and in his heyday he amassed approximately 10,000 students, of which 32 were the highest samurai rank of *daimyō*. The techniques of his school were few: in fact, the original curriculum of Mugai-ryū consists of a mere 10 long-sword and 3 short-sword techniques. Tactics for duels and iaijutsu were also added later on, but the original ones developed by Gettan were simple but effective. This may be one of the reasons why his school became so popular, but his emphasis on the mind was also surely a factor.

His style of *kenjutsu* was very much a path to enlightenment in its own right, and one of his famous Zen teachings was that of *"Sara ni sanze yo sanjū-nen"* which roughly translates to "Do it again, another thirty years." Thirty years was considered the traditional period for ascetic training. Of course, this was just a figure of speech, but Gettan's point here is that once that's finished, however, you have to start again. There is no end to walking the One True Way.

Guidelines to
Kendo Promotional Examinations
Part 2   By Jeff Marsten (Kendo Kyōshi 7-dan)

Gradings linger in the shadow of shiai
If this is so, then all future hope is lost
Winning is here today and gone tomorrow
Yet development has no end.
— Tanka Poem

Part 1 of this article was featured in *Kendo World* 8.3 and discussed the history and purpose of grading and ways in which to improve them. Part 2 will focus on the actual criteria used in a grading.

POINTS TO BE OBSERVED

What follows is an example of what examiners should look to make their evaluation and final decision within the allotted time.

KYŪ

1. *Chakusō* (appearance)
2. *Reihō* (manners/etiquette)
3. *Shisei* (posture)
4. *Kamae-kata* (correct *kamae*)
5. *Ashi-sabaki* (footwork)
6. *Kiai/kakegoe* (vocalisation)

7. *Kihon datotsu* (basic strikes)
8. *Maai* (maintaining a proper distance from opponent)
9. *Zanshin* (continued mental alertness after a strike)

YŪDANSHA

In addition to items 1–9 stated above for *kyū* grades, *yūdansha* should also be examined on:

10. *Ki-ken-tai-itchi* (striking with a unification of spirit, sword, and body)
11. *Datotsu no kikai* (striking opportunities)
12. *Yūkō*-datotsu, *renzoku-waza*, *ōji-waza*, *shikake-waza*

KATA

1. *Shisei*
2. *kamae*
3. *Ashi-sabaki*
4. *Kiai*
5. Accuracy of cut
6. *Maai*
7. *Zanshin*
8. *Riai*
9. *Uchidachi* vs. *Shidachi*
10. *Metsuke*

APPEARANCE

Even before "*Hajime!*" is called to start the practical component of the exam, the judges should have already started to grade the candidate. Indeed, before the candidate has even assumed *chūdan-no-kamae*, the grading panel should already be aware of some of the aspects of the individual's level of kendo. If a candidate has a poor or sub-standard *kamae*, their kendo will also be flawed. A sub-standard *kamae* indicates that there are probably problems with footwork and/or striking. Also, kenshi at each level must demonstrate a degree of dignity and presence appropriate for the rank being tested. For lower grades, this may only be wearing the uniform and equipment correctly.

Hakama: The length of the *hakama* should be so the front touches the top of the foot with the back slightly higher and covering the ankle. The *koshi-ita* (the panel at the back of the *hakama*) should flat against the small of the back. The *himo* should be tied in a square knot and the ends tucked into waist. The *hakama* pleats should be straight as they represent the samurai virtues of *jin* (humanity), *gi* (justice), *rei* (courtesy), *chi* (knowledge) and *shin* (trust).

Tenugui: The *tenugui* should be worn so that there is no part sticking out of the back of the *men*. It should not be so low on the forehead that it is visible through the *men-gane*. Do not place a folded *tenugui* in the chin rest if the *men* is too big – a special pad is made for that purpose, and goes between the top of the head and the underside of the top of the *men*. Children will often use a *men* that is too big, so they should inset a pad to make it fit. This gives the child better protection, and also eliminates the use of an unsightly *tenugui* in the chin area, which often falls out during *keiko*.

Men-himo: The *men-himo* should be tied in a bow (*chō-musubi*), be straight, and look as if they are one cord, not several. The ends and loops should all be the same length and not exceed 40cm.

Dō-himo: The upper *dō-himo* should be tied with the ends tucked in behind the *mune*, not dangling in front. The lower *dō-himo* should be horizontal and tied in a bow.

Tare-himo: The *tare-himo* should be flat and run across the *koshi-ita* at the back, and not make the ōdare bulge at the front. Tuck the *tare-himo* under the band, not just behind the front panel.

Kote-himo: The *kote-himo* should not be frayed or hang down. If they are too long, cut them off and wrap the ends (before cutting) with ½" strapping tape. Seal the ends with a drop of super glue.

REIGI (ETIQUETTE)

It is said that kendo begins and ends with *rei*, so a natural place for this guide to start is with a discussion of *reigi*. The physical manifestation of *reigi* (etiquette) is represented by a *rei* (bow) as one enters the dojo or *shiai-jō*. Thus each practice or match starts with a display of respect for the venue and the other practitioners. It also shows that the individual is ready to learn. *Rei* is the act of casting aside the ego and opening the mind to learning without questioning everything. The end is signalled by repeating the process and thanking everyone for the practice when leaving the dojo. The natural outcome of this is that the same manners should carry over into all aspects of the practitioner's life. The *reigi* of kendo is correct behaviour in all dealings with other people as you work through your daily activities. A failure in this behaviour is a moral failure in the kenshi's character and training.

At the practical level, kendo is a discipline in which the purpose is to defeat the opponent both mentally and physically. Without the rules governing etiquette from start to finish, kendo degenerates into an act of merely bashing the opponent to win by any means possible. Kendo supported by *reigi* remains an art in which the objective is to overcome the self. One should be "thankful" to one's partner for striking you and exposing your weaknesses as this offers you clues for improvement. Practice is an exchange of techniques, and the kenshi must be polite to the person "giving" you such a gift.

What follows is a list of examination criteria that can be used by both examiners and examinees. It is provided by the International Kendo Federation (FIK).

JITSUGI

During the *jitsugi* component of the examination the following points should be observed by the examiners:

Rei: Is the opening *rei* to the opponent done properly?

Shinai: Is the *shinai* at *sagetō* during the *rei*, and then lifted to *taitō* as each kenshi advances into the court? The *shinai* should have the *nakayui* tied in the proper place—a quarter of the *shinai's* length from the *kensen*.

Ashi-sabaki: The footwork as the candidate advances onto the court should be smooth, sliding steps with the toes down.

Nuki-tō: The drawing of the sword should be in the *kesa-giri* manner as each kenshi starts their third step.

Sonkyo: The back should be straight with the elbows not touching the thighs.

Kensen: The *kensen* should point at the opponent's throat.

Grip: The left hand should grip the *tsuka* at the bottom, and the right hand near the *tsuba*.

Kamae: Correct posture, standing up straight, feet positioned correctly, *shinai* tip at the correct level. *Shinai* held correctly, particularly for *ikkyū* and above.

Maai: Is the candidate maintaining proper distance—*issoku-ittō-no-maai*, the one-step, one-cut interval?

Uchi: Is the quality of the strike—focus, power, accuracy—suitable for the level being examined? As a point of reference, would the strike be *yūkō-datotsu* for that division in *shiai*? Is the candidate striking with the *datotsu-bu*, or are they consistently off target?

Sae: Proper use of the hands—*tenouchi* (grip), *teko* (leverage), both hands striking together at the same time.

Seme: Pressure. Applying offensive pressure on the opponent becomes important from 4-dan level. Up to 3-dan is about showing a mastery of basics.

Riai-kikai: Reasons and logic for attacking. Is there an opening? Did the candidate create the opening? This is especially important for the upper *dan* grades, especially 5-dan and above.

Kime: Did the candidate maintain contact and engagement after the strike? This should be demonstrated at 3-dan.

Jitsugi: Does the *jitsugi* meet the expectations of the level being examined? Care should be taken by examiners not to use individuals that are above the assessed level as the benchmark.

At each successive level, the ability to know when to attack and recognise correct opportunities to do so will determine success in the examination. Simply attacking indiscriminately, rather than when openings manifest, will result in poor strikes. That is not to say that you should be defensive; it is said that kendo is 50% offence and 50% defence. However, offence is the half that carries more weight. Defensive striking is marked down while even unsuccessful offensive attacks executed with a positive spirit that result in

ai-uchi (simultaneous strikes by both opponents) will be a plus. Opportunities can be created in a number of ways, and you need to study this well during *keiko*. Only through constant *keiko* is the required knowledge for kendo examinations acquired. There is no substitute for practice, and there are no silver bullets. Other factors in the *jitsugi* component are good *kiai* and *ki-ken-tai-itchi*, *seme*, *sutemi* and *zanshin*.

KYŪ CRITERIA

There are no formal criteria established at a national level either in the United States or Japan for the levels below *ikkyū*. Each regional federation must establish their own to insure a uniform and consistent grading process. In Japan, the *kyū* grades were established to help children progress, and they are awarded at the dojo level in many cases, and may not even have any testing criteria. When kendo migrated out of Japan the *kyū* system was applied in different ways. In the United States, the thinking was that because we do not practise every day and have adult beginners, a motivational method for progression was necessary. Hence the *kyū* system was applied to both adults and children after the resumption of kendo in the early 1950s. At the time in Japan, it was rare to see an adult beginner—only children started kendo. Now many adults in Japan are taking up kendo, but because of the overwhelming number of high *dan*, it is not a problem to start them at the *ikkyū* level. This, however, is not the case outside Japan.

From 6-*kyū* through to 2-*kyū* can be awarded by the dojo depending on the regional federation. Other federations formally test for these grades, and some have age restrictions for children. *Ikkyū* and above should always be done through the formal examination process. While it is normal to have both adults and children testing for the same *kyū* level, there can be a great deal of difference in the basic skill level between them. Children may have been doing kendo longer, and have much better basics. When the mental maturity of the adults is factored in, however, an experienced examiner will understand this and grade accordingly.

If an examination board tries to grade them as equivalents, myriad problems arise. First, children improve in the basics more readily. By the time both are grading for 3-*kyū*, children are generally much better than adults. However, the children do not have life experience, nor do they have the same physical strength. While the *katana* is a great equaliser, the *shinai* is not necessarily. Thus, we see differences in skill level between an adult 3-*kyū* and a 12-year-old 3-*kyū*. If we reflect on the reality of dojo here in the United States where an *ikkyū* or *shodan* may be the "sensei", then certainly we do not want a 14- or 15-year-old running the dojo. Kendo is not just about hitting someone with a stick. The *kyū* grades provide time for the adult beginner to learn kendo basics and etiquette. Moreover, another important meaning for *kyū* grades is to allow for steady progress of the juniors. What do you do with a 12-year-old *ikkyū* for the next two to three years until they are eligible for *shodan*?

As you will see in the criteria for *shodan*, the years prior to reaching this level are for this purpose, and must be in place before that grade can be awarded.

These are recommendations (not rules) for a candidate's minimum grading age:
6-kyū: 9-years-old, *5-kyū*: 10, *4-kyū*: 11, *3-kyū*: 12, *2-kyū*: 13*I, kkyū*: 14, *Shodan*: 15 (AUSKF/FIK regulations require a candidate to be at least 14 for *shodan*).

I would not recommend starting anyone above *3-kyū* for their first examination. If a person tests every six months, this would allow a couple of years for them to develop the appropriate understanding of *reigi* and *reihō* in their kendo. It is also undesirable for a *shodan* with only six months experience to launch a dojo. This does happen, but if the federation cares about the future development of both the individual and the organisation, then a dojo instructor should be at least 3-dan and 18-years of age. This is to achieve a certain level of maturity to handle the responsibility that goes with rank.

8-KYŪ:

By dojo discretion—suggested skills:
1. Display proper *reigi*, cleaning of dojo, proper bows and addressing of instructors and senior students. *Dōgu* not required.
2. Knowledge of basic commands: *kamae, sonkyo, seiza, rei, mokusō, hajime, yame*.
3. Perform basic footwork: *okuriashi*.4. Perform *suburi*.
5. Able to do *uchikomi*. Make basic *kote* and *men* strikes against someone holding a *shinai*.

7-KYŪ:

By dojo discretion, suggested skills.
1. Same requirements as *6-kyū*.
2. Perform basic strikes: *kote, men*, and *dō*.
3. Able to do *kirikaeshi* (not graded on receiving).

NOTE: For ranks 6-*kyū* to 3-*kyū*, basic strikes and drills will be performed and graded as part of the examination.

6-KYŪ:

Primarily a children's rank. Its purpose is to encourage them to stay in kendo.
1. Show improved skills of all lower rank requirements.
2. Put on and fold up their *dōgi*. (Not graded, recommended.)
3. Put on *dōgu* without assistance.
4. Perform basic footwork—*ashi-sabaki*.
5. Perform *kirikaeshi, kote, men*, and *dō, kihon datotsu*.
6. Able to do *kakari-geiko* with *motodachi*.
7. Able to begin and end *keiko* properly (*reihō*).

5-KYŪ:

1. Show improved basic skills above the *6-kyū* level. Minimum age 10.

4-KYŪ:

Primarily a children's rank. Its purpose is to encourage them to stay in kendo.
1. Show improved basic skills above the *5-kyū*. Minimum age 11.
2. *Ashi-sabaki*.
3. *Chakusō*: *Himo* tied correctly (not hanging loose).4. *Kihon* basics improved, especially footwork.
5. *Kakari-geiko, kakegoe* (vocalisation) and *kiai* (showing a good spirit).
6. *Reihō*: Able to enter and leave the court correctly.

3-KYŪ:

Adults and children. Minimum age 12 with more than one year of practice. Highest starting rank for a first grading.
1. *Kamae*: The candidate demonstrates a correct *kamae*.

2. *Shisei*: The candidate stands up straight, back foot not turned out.
3. *Ashi-sabaki*: No walking after a strike.
4. *Zanshin*: Following through after a strike.
5. Strong *kiai*.
6. *Chakuso*: Is the *dōgu* worn correctly including *hakama* and *kendōgi*? (A short *hakama* is acceptable for juniors.)
7. *Kihon datotsu*: Does the candidate make valid strikes.

2-KYŪ:

Adults and children. Minimum age 13 with more than two years of practice.
1. *Kamae*: The candidate demonstrates a correct *kamae*.
2. *Shisei*: The candidate stands up straight, back foot not turned out.
3. *Ashi-sabaki*: No walking after a strike.
4. *Zanshin*: Following through after a strike.
5. Strong *kiai*.
6. *Chakuso*: Is the *dōgu* worn correctly including *hakama* and *kendōgi*?

IKKYŪ:

Adults and children, minimum age 14, will be ready for *shodan* within a year.
1. *Reihō, men-himo, dō-himo*, correct *hakama* length (juniors excluded)
2. *Shinai*: *Nakayui* and *tsuba* positioned correctly.
3. *Ritsurei*: Maintain eye contact, posture correct (bend at waist, 15 degrees).
4. Back straight in *sonkyo*.
5. Correct grip on *shinai*.
6. *Kensen* at correct height
7. Show ability to properly grip the *shinai*.
8. Position of feet correct: left foot pointing forward
9. *Ashi-sabaki*: No walking after a strike. 10. Strong *kiai*. 11. Lifts both hands up- no right hand only on datotsu
12. Stretch out arms after a strike.
13. Some *renzoku-waza* (at least *kote-men*).
14. *Maai* at a reasonable distance.
15. Act as a *motodachi*.
16. *Kata*: No major mistakes in sequence and form.

DAN CRITERIA

If adjudicating as *shinpan* in a *shodan* level *shiai* and you judge a strike as *yūkō-datotsu*, can it actually be worth more than that? By that, I mean "closer to an *ippon*." So, what is the difference between an *ippon* and a *yūkō-datotsu*?

A *yūkō-datotsu* requires a lesser degree of perfection than an *ippon* and is a convention that allows a tournament to function. An *ippon* is defined as the culmination of *sutemi* and *jiri-itchi* (technique and theory in unison). You win mentally and then physically with a single blow, perceiving when the opponent wants to strike and then defeating them before they can. This includes the concepts of *san-sappō* (kill the sword, technique, and spirit) and *mittsu-no-sen* (the three initiatives).

Furthermore, consider the relevance to *kata*: what is the underlying technique and theory? Are the strikes *shikake-* or *ōji-waza*? Whether or not an individual can demonstrate and actually use *ōji-waza* is determined by the limited time in a grading, as well as if the opponent provides an opportunity, which they might not do. This means that the examiner must also consider the opponent's kendo as if one person performs poorly, their actions can affect the other.

The mindset of the examiners can be at polar opposites, ranging from "Everyone fails unless the examinee proves different" or "Everyone passes unless the examinee fails themselves by being unable to meet the criteria required for the rank". Questions the examiner must ask themselves are, "Is there a fatal flaw in the examinees basics?"; "If there are problems, can they be easily fixed?" "Will the individual be worthy of the rank within six months? i.e. the individual is at the bottom of the ladder and will grow into the rank." "Will this growth occur during the waiting period for the next rank?"

These questions raise the spectre of validity and reliability. Are the results graded on a curve, and different for each exam because of the group? Does this occur even within an exam from level to level because there is an individual that raises the curve? If the exam is graded on a curve, then the results are skewed and the process is called into question by the very individuals it is meant to serve.

Just as one group of *shinpan* can raise or lower the bar on what is *yūkō-datotsu* within a *shiai* division, so can the *shinsa-in* in a grading. When this happens, the process is neither reliable or valid.

Therefore, the *shinsa-in* must have a common understanding of what constitutes the criteria for each level being graded. This does not mean to advocate for lowering the bar, but rather dictates that controls be put into the process. Such controls are:

1. A grading sheet that provides a consistent method of reliability.
2. Regular training of *shinsa-in*.
3. Monitoring of *shinsa-in* that fall out of the norm, e.g. failing or passing everyone. If the variance in results is large when compared to the group as a whole, then steps must be taken to improve examiner skills.

The following are descriptions of the requirements for the different *dan* grades that have been determined by the FIK:

SHODAN

Basic skills at a sufficient level. This means that footwork, swing and striking are developed enough that the individual can now progress to the higher levels, and that they understand the opportunity and *riai* of making an attack.

2-DAN

Basic skills (*waza*, etc.) at a satisfactory level. The candidate can demonstrate ability in *shikake-waza*, *harai-waza*, *debana-waza*, *hiki-waza*, and *ōji-waza*. The occasion may not arise for the candidate to use most of these *waza*, but the candidate should demonstrate better basics than at the *shodan* level and be able to use a greater variety of techniques. The candidate at this level should not be obsessed with the use of *waza*, but should start to master creating the opportunity to attack. Cuts should have a good vertical motion with the use of both hands and *tenouchi*.

3-DAN

Solid basics, superior skills use *seme* and *kensen* to initiate attacks and have sharp *waza*. Particularly the use of *ōji-waza* should be incorporated in the candidate's kendo.

4-DAN

Fully acquired basics and applications with superior skills. The candidate should display solid kendo and *kamae*, display mastery of a variety of techniques, *yūkō-datotsu*, excellent footwork and posture. An attacking *kamae* full of energy should be displayed rather than a waiting *kamae* that reacts to the opponent.

5-DAN

Well acquired basics and applications with excellent skills. Starting with the 5-dan examination, the candidate must truly exhibit the use of *seme* and *kensen* to create the moment of attack. Often failure is caused by the candidate doing *shiai* style of *keiko* and trying to win points. One must demonstrate control of the centre, the opponent's spirit, as well as have mastery of footwork and *shinai* manipulation. The kendo displayed must be logical without unnecessary strikes and actions. Strikes are followed by *zanshin* that demonstrate true mental alertness.

6-DAN

Profound knowledge of kendo principles. Skills the same as at the 5-dan level, but even more *riai* must be demonstrated. The candidate should demonstrate a strong control of the centre, efficient use of *waza* and footwork, and have mental control of the opponent and situation.

7-DAN

Fully acquired and profound knowledge of principles with outstanding skills. (These are demonstrated by *kamae*, *seme*, *riai* and movement.) All aspects of the previous ranks must be present and an essence of dignity that speaks of quality kendo. This dignity should show both on and off the court in the person's life.

8-DAN

Fully acquired profound knowledge of principles with perfect skills

KŌDANSHA EXAMS

"Kendo is the path to defining character through sword training." Regarding the laws of kendo, it is imperative to study kendo by training in accordance with the ideal of kendo or one will not be able to achieve the level of *kōdansha*. One aspect of this is demonstrating "*jiri-itchi*": the unification of theory and practice (mind and body unified). As defined by the Kendo Dictionary "*ji*" means "technique" and "*ri*" theory. The precept that it is important to train in such a way as to unify technique and theory. The aim of this precept is a search for truth by the realisation of the functions of mind and body through training in techniques.

PROCESS IMPROVEMENT

From reading articles written in the Europe Zone, it is clear to see that the problems highlighted above also exist there. Outside of kendo, in successful manufacturing companies for example, the use of quality circles and continual process improvement that follow Japanese methods have been implemented. This means you develop a standardised process and address problem areas. "We've always done it this way" does not work, and neither does tribal knowledge. There are too many variables and personal opinions passed down with these problem-solving methods because they do not in actuality solve problems. If Olympic coaches and trainers used this methodology, no records could ever be broken.

Consider the waiting period between ranks. The individual needs to ask what am I doing to prepare, change and improve to reach the next level? Kendo is a process that could be thought of as a four-legged stool. *Kata, keiko, shinsa,* and *shiai* are the legs, and if one of them is broken, you fall over. It is not about becoming a champion in *shiai*, but quality in the overall process is what is important. Therefore, the process must be valid, reliable and measurable.

FINAL THOUGHTS

How is being a *shinpan* and being a *shinsa-in* related? Depending on what kendo federation you are a member of, as a 4-dan you could be asked to serve as a *shinsa-in* and certainly as a *shinpan*. So, if you are grading a *kyū* examination, it could be for both children and adults. The same could be true when serving as a *shinpan*.

If your federation has laid out the requirements for

2-*kyū* and below, you have directions on how to perform the task. In addition to the requirements there should be training and level setting for the *shinsa-in*. If a federation assigns a person as a *shinsa-in* without any training then the system lacks reliability and consequently validity. Furthermore, if every time you have an exam the criteria changes there is no validity.

The membership needs to be cognizant of these requirements so they can see the results as valid. When this is not the case then every exam is questionable because there is too much variability within the results. Consistent measuring of the results and identifying *shinsa-in* outside the norm provides a tool to attain reliability. Those *shinsa-in* whose judgements continually fall outside of the mean need to be made aware of this. If they fail or pass everyone their results are out of line with the other *shinsa-in* and the federation must take corrective action. This means that the federation must have clear guidelines and criteria that make the exam process valid, reliable and measurable. This also means that the club leaders within the federation must provide correct instruction and preparation for those testing.

Just as you cannot inspect quality into a manufacturing process, the *shinsa-in* cannot grade quality into the examinees. This quality must be built at the club/dojo level. To accomplish this, the training and education of *shinsa-in* must include the sensei teaching and developing the students. This will give long-term benefits to the entire organisation and not just the *shinsa-in*. Student and teacher alike need to understand and accept that the test results are valid. So just as in a *shiai* where the *shinpan* call points that are understood by the competitors, other *shinpan* and audience, so must the *shinsa* results make sense to those testing, the examinees' sensei, and the *shinsa-in* as a board of examiners. Therefore, if we look at what is *yūkō-datotsu* for *shiai*, it should basically be the same for *shinsa*. There should not, and cannot, be very different standards for both. The point of these articles has been twofold:

1. To encourage examining organisations to improve their process by putting emphasis on the training of examiners. To provide a means

and methodology toward standardisation that emphasizes reliability, measurability and validity with the equal amount of effort that is put into *shinpan* and *shiai*.

2. To help the individual understand what is required for each level. By understanding the requirements, they can better prepare a plan of self-direction toward their goal.

Finally, it is critical that organisations adapt an overall approach to quality improvement. The leadership of an organisation should be thinking about how to measure the functions they that provide. By establishing standards of excellence, the organisation's value increases and it becomes more than just a dues collector.

What are some of the ways in which the organisation can be measured?

Success at major events, i.e., how well the organisation performs at a national championship level tournament; the pass rate at the *kōdansha* level if it is a national examination (this same measurement can be used at the club level with regard to regional examinations, provided the regional test meets criteria outlined above); and attendance at seminars for the application of the principles of kendo, *shinpan*, and *shiai*. In short does the organisation fulfil its stated goals.

How is this fulfilment measured? In general, amongst the population of any organisation are individual kenshi with skill sets outside of kendo. These skill sets can be utilised through a volunteer program to bring non-kendo knowledge and skills in the organisation that can and will improve it. If the kendo organisation has a mission statement that is continually applied and activities are vetted with regard to that mission, it will flourish and grow. Consequently, the quality of kendo will continually improve.

"We have always done it that way" is not a good enough system for improvement. As in *mitori-geiko*, we should steal the *waza* of other organisations, not just of kendo, but also from Olympic sports, process improvement methodology, process engineering, and sports science. Build a better stool, but make the *shinsa* leg especially strong.

BUSHIDO EXPLAINED

The Japanese Samurai Code:
A New Interpretation

By Alex Bennett

Illustrations by Baptiste Tavernier

Arguably the most celebrated warrior in Japanese history, Miyamoto Musashi (1582–1645) was born in Harima as the second son of Tahara Iesada. He had his first taste of combat at the age of thirteen when he challenged and killed Arima Kihei of the Shinto-ryu. He spent the next fifteen years as an itinerant swordsman dueling his way to notoriety. Musashi established the Enmei-ryu school in 1605. He renamed his style of swordsmanship Nito Ichi-ryu ("The School of Two Swords as One"), and finally Niten Ichi-ryu ("Two Heavens One School") because "all warriors, from general to rank-and-file, are duty bound to wear two swords in their belts," so warriors must know the merits of carrying two swords.

The best-known of his sixty odd duels was in 1610 against Ganryu Kojiro on an island called Funajima (later called Ganryujima). After defeating Kojiro, he realized that his success and survival thus far were due more to luck than to any genuine knowledge. He decided to spend the rest of his life in pursuit of a greater truth, and after many years of austere training came to understand that the principles

for success in combat are the same as for all aspects of life.

Musashi is credited with several books related to the martial arts, including *Heidokyo* (1605), *Heiho Kakitsuke* (1638), *Heiho Sanjugo-kajo* (1641), *Dokkodo*

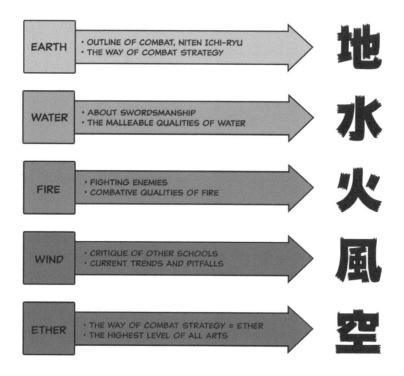

EARTH
- OUTLINE OF COMBAT, NITEN ICHI-RYU
- THE WAY OF COMBAT STRATEGY

地

WATER
- ABOUT SWORDSMANSHIP
- THE MALLEABLE QUALITIES OF WATER

水

FIRE
- FIGHTING ENEMIES
- COMBATIVE QUALITIES OF FIRE

火

WIND
- CRITIQUE OF OTHER SCHOOLS
- CURRENT TRENDS AND PITFALLS

風

ETHER
- THE WAY OF COMBAT STRATEGY = ETHER
- THE HIGHEST LEVEL OF ALL ARTS

空

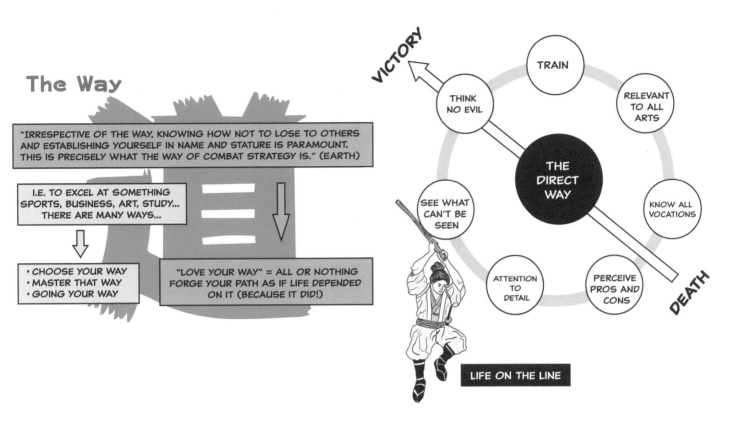

The Way

"IRRESPECTIVE OF THE WAY, KNOWING HOW NOT TO LOSE TO OTHERS AND ESTABLISHING YOURSELF IN NAME AND STATURE IS PARAMOUNT. THIS IS PRECISELY WHAT THE WAY OF COMBAT STRATEGY IS." (EARTH)

I.E. TO EXCEL AT SOMETHING SPORTS, BUSINESS, ART, STUDY... THERE ARE MANY WAYS...

• CHOOSE YOUR WAY
• MASTER THAT WAY
• GOING YOUR WAY

"LOVE YOUR WAY" = ALL OR NOTHING FORGE YOUR PATH AS IF LIFE DEPENDED ON IT (BECAUSE IT DID!)

VICTORY

TRAIN

THINK NO EVIL

RELEVANT TO ALL ARTS

THE DIRECT WAY

SEE WHAT CAN'T BE SEEN

KNOW ALL VOCATIONS

ATTENTION TO DETAIL

PERCEIVE PROS AND CONS

DEATH

LIFE ON THE LINE

(1645), and the most famous of all, *Gorin-no-Sho* (1645) which he wrote for his

students in Kumamoto's Reigando cave, handing it over one week before he died.

Gorin-no-sho (Book of Five Rings) consists of five chapters or "scrolls": Chi (earth), Sui (water), Ka (fire), Fu (wind), and Ku (Ether). In the Earth scroll, Musashi documents the first half of his life. He also includes an introduction to military tactics and the philosophy behind the school he created. In the Water scroll, Musashi explains various aspects of individual combat, such as mental and physical posture, gaze, manipulating the sword, footwork, and fighting stances.

In Fire, he expounds how to choose the best site for dueling, how to control the enemy by taking the initiative, and how to implement strategies.

In the fourth scroll, Wind, he critiques other schools of swordsmanship and outlines their weaknesses. Ether is a short but decidedly complicated section where Musashi delves into how he developed the Niten Ichi-ryu. He discloses the supreme level of combat and all arts by referring to the allegorical "void." "Having comprehended the truth of the Way, you can then let it go. You will find liberation in the Way of combat strategy and naturally attain a

marvelous capacity to know the most rational rhythm for every moment. Your strike will manifest on its own and hit the target on its own. All this represents the Way of the Ether."

Musashi taught that in the "Way of combat strategy," overlooking the most fundamental matters will hold the warrior back. By dedicating all of his energies to learning swordsmanship via the "Direct Way," the warrior will learn to "defeat men through superior technique, and even beat them just by looking with your eyes. Your body will learn to move freely through the rigors of arduous training and you will also overcome your opponent physically. Furthermore, with your spirit attuned to the Way you will triumph over the enemy with your mind. Having come so far, how can you be beaten by anyone?"

He observed that in the practice of all arts, struggling in the pursuit of the true Way, allowing one's mind to wander even a little, leads to a colossal deviation. "Inquiring into the minds of samurai today, it would seem that many believe the warrior's Way demands nothing more than an unwavering preparedness for death."

Musashi contends that all people are prepared to sacrifice their life when the time comes. The only difference in the warrior's Way compared to others is that

The Perils of Being Negligent

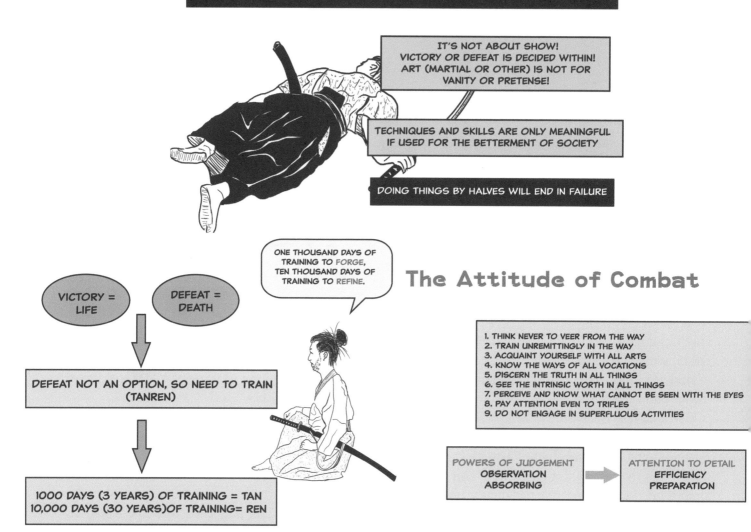

COLORFUL DISPLAYS OF TECHNIQUE ARE FLAUNTED IN THESE [FALSE] MARTIAL ART "WAYS" TO FORCE THE FLOWER INTO BLOOM. PROFITEERS BLATHERING OVER THIS DOJO OR THAT DOJO, TEACHING ONE WAY OR LEARNING ANOTHER IN THE HOPE OF CONQUERING IN THE FRAY, FITS THE [POPULAR] ADAGE "UNRIPE MARTIAL ARTS ARE THE ROOT OF SERIOUS HARM. (EARTH)

IT'S NOT ABOUT SHOW! VICTORY OR DEFEAT IS DECIDED WITHIN! ART (MARTIAL OR OTHER) IS NOT FOR VANITY OR PRETENSE!

TECHNIQUES AND SKILLS ARE ONLY MEANINGFUL IF USED FOR THE BETTERMENT OF SOCIETY

DOING THINGS BY HALVES WILL END IN FAILURE

ONE THOUSAND DAYS OF TRAINING TO FORGE, TEN THOUSAND DAYS OF TRAINING TO REFINE.

The Attitude of Combat

VICTORY = LIFE

DEFEAT = DEATH

DEFEAT NOT AN OPTION, SO NEED TO TRAIN (TANREN)

1000 DAYS (3 YEARS) OF TRAINING = TAN
10,000 DAYS (30 YEARS) OF TRAINING= REN

1. THINK NEVER TO VEER FROM THE WAY
2. TRAIN UNREMITTINGLY IN THE WAY
3. ACQUAINT YOURSELF WITH ALL ARTS
4. KNOW THE WAYS OF ALL VOCATIONS
5. DISCERN THE TRUTH IN ALL THINGS
6. SEE THE INTRINSIC WORTH IN ALL THINGS
7. PERCEIVE AND KNOW WHAT CANNOT BE SEEN WITH THE EYES
8. PAY ATTENTION EVEN TO TRIFLES
9. DO NOT ENGAGE IN SUPERFLUOUS ACTIVITIES

POWERS OF JUDGEMENT
OBSERVATION
ABSORBING

ATTENTION TO DETAIL
EFFICIENCY
PREPARATION

the "warrior must win." There are no second chances.

When Musashi wrote *Gorin-no-sho*, the country had not seen war for over a decade, and there was thus a generation of samurai who had never experienced battle first hand. Perhaps this was an admonition to his students that true mortal combat was not something to be understood conceptually, and therefore unfounded arrogance in such matters would lead them down the wrong path. The important thing was to engage with single-minded resolve. The ability to do this would open the mind to a profound understanding of all things.

Musashi was relentless in his own study and urged his students to be patient "Looking In" and "Looking At" as they learned the virtue of all phenomena "utilizing every opportunity to accumulate actual experience" as they traverse "the thousand-mile road one step at a time." He advised there was no need for haste in training, but instead "seek victory today over the self of yesterday," mindful of keeping strictly to the path. "Even if you defeat the most daunting of adversaries, if your victories are not in accord with the principles contained within these scrolls, then they cannot be considered true to the Way." It was through embracing the principles of the Way that the swordsman could prevail over dozens of men. Mastering the art of combat for individual duels was the same as that of large-scale strategy for battle. But

"Looking In" and "Looking At"

ONE'S GAZE SHOULD BE EXPANSIVE AND FAR-REACHING. THIS IS THE DUAL GAZE OF "LOOKING IN" (KAN) AND "LOOKING AT" (KEN). THE GAZE FOR "LOOKING IN" IS INTENSE WHEREAS THAT FOR "LOOKING AT" IS GENTLE. IT IS OF UTMOST IMPORTANCE FOR A WARRIOR TO SEE DISTANT THINGS AS IF THEY WERE CLOSE AND CLOSE THINGS AS IF THEY WERE DISTANT. (WATER)

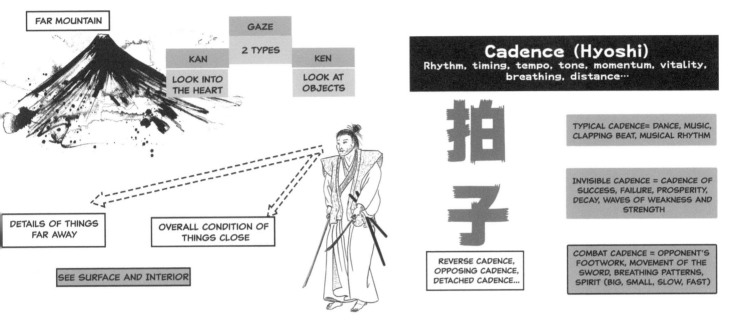

FAR MOUNTAIN

GAZE
2 TYPES

KAN — LOOK INTO THE HEART

KEN — LOOK AT OBJECTS

DETAILS OF THINGS FAR AWAY

OVERALL CONDITION OF THINGS CLOSE

SEE SURFACE AND INTERIOR

Cadence (Hyoshi)
Rhythm, timing, tempo, tone, momentum, vitality, breathing, distance…

拍子

TYPICAL CADENCE= DANCE, MUSIC, CLAPPING BEAT, MUSICAL RHYTHM

INVISIBLE CADENCE = CADENCE OF SUCCESS, FAILURE, PROSPERITY, DECAY, WAVES OF WEAKNESS AND STRENGTH

REVERSE CADENCE, OPPOSING CADENCE, DETACHED CADENCE…

COMBAT CADENCE = OPPONENT'S FOOTWORK, MOVEMENT OF THE SWORD, BREATHING PATTERNS, SPIRIT (BIG, SMALL, SLOW, FAST)

this took time. "One-thousand days of training to forge, ten-thousand days of training to refine."

The correct attitude in the Way of combat must be no different from one's normal state of mind. "In the course of your daily life, and when engaged in strategy, there should be no change whatsoever in your outlook. Your mind should be expansive and direct, devoid of tension, but not at all casual," that is, keep the mind centered, "swaying serenely and freely so that it does not come to a standstill in moments of change."

Musashi is very matter of fact in his technical explanations. He also emphasizes psychological details and the importance of powers of concentration and the ability to observe all things unimpeded. "The swordsman must learn to polish the two layers of his mind." Musashi explains these layers as the "heart of perception" and the "heart of intent," the two gazes of *kan* ("looking in") and *ken* ("looking at"). One's gaze should be expansive and far-reaching. This is the dual gaze of "looking in" and "looking at." It is as if one is looking at something close to you as a mountain far away, taking in its entire shape while perceiving something that is far away as if it were very close.

The gaze for "looking in" is intense whereas that for "looking at" is gentle. "It is of utmost importance

for a warrior to see distant things as if they were close and close things as if they were distant." It is vital to be able to see both without needing to move the eyes.

Central to Musashi's swordsmanship was using this perception to identify the rhythm inherent in all things. "First, the warrior must know the cadence of harmony and then learn those of discord. He must know the striking, interval and counter cadences that manifest among big and small, fast and slow rhythms."

He declares how it is critical for success to know how to adopt "counter rhythms" to what the enemy is doing. "You must discern cadences of various enemies and employ a rhythm that is unexpected to them. Use your wisdom to detect and strike concealed cadences to seize victory."

Musashi states he was about fifty when he realized the true meaning of the Way. "Having attained the essence of the Way of combat strategy, I practice the disciplines of many arts without the need of a teacher in any of them." Indeed, Musashi was a talented artist, and some of his paintings remain today in Japan as National Treasures. He attributes this to tapping the "Ether," a place where there is nothing. "I consider this emptiness as something which cannot be known.

- THOROUGHLY KNOW THE WAY OF COMBAT STRATEGY
- KNOW VARIOUS ARTS
- A MIND THAT NEVER WAIVERS
- POLISH THE TWO LAYERS OF THE MIND, "HEART OF PERCEPTION" AND "HEART OF INTENT""
- "LOOK IN" (WITH THE HEART) AND "LOOK AT" (WITH THE EYES)

THERE IS *GOOD*, NOT EVIL IN THE ETHER
THERE IS WISDOM, THERE IS REASON
THERE IS THE WAY, THE MIND, EMPTY

 ETHER

A PLACE WHERE THERE IS NOTHING

CLOUDS OF CONFUSION

WHEN THE SPIRIT IS UNCURLED AND COMPARED WITH OVERARCHING UNIVERSAL PRINCIPLES, IT BECOMES EVIDENT THAT A PREJUDICED MIND AND A DISTORTED VIEW OF THINGS HAVE LED TO A DEPARTURE FROM THE PROPER PATH.

Of course, Ether is also nothing. Knowing what does exist, one can then know what does not." Ether is not something that cannot be distinguished, nor is it a description of various doubts that are harbored in the mind. By scrupulously learning by heart the Way of combat strategy and thoroughly studying other martial arts without forgoing any aspect related to the practice of the warrior's Way, the samurai must seek to "put the Way into practice each hour of every day without tiring or losing focus." Only then can the true Ether become apparent, "where all the clouds of confusion have completely lifted, leaving not a hint of haziness."

As his final teaching, he implores his students to "Make the sincere heart your Way as you practice strategy in its broadest sense, correctly and lucidly. Ponder the Ether as you study the Way. As you practice the Way, the Ether will open before you."

There is Good, not Evil in the Ether
There is Wisdom
There is Reason
There is the Way
The Mind, Empty

How do Musashi's ideals relate to modern kendo. How can his philosophy be applied to, for example,

success in *shiai*? The following is a brief sample of things that I pondered while tranlsating his text, *Gorin-no-sho*. Note that there are many more possibilities, but that is a book in its own right. In this article I will look at two scenarios: what happens when the opponent's cadence is disturbed, and the significance of "winning the place" and how this affects the opponent's actions.

Example 1. DISTURBED CADENCE

When you move in to apply pressure on your opponent and...

1. *Opponent steps back, sword down, body leaning backwards = Back heel on the floor.*
↓
Opponent can't attack. Only thinking of defending = Striking chance

2. *Opponent steps back, sword up, hands slightly raised = Opponent can't attack strongly. Can only strike with hands. Will try to avoid your attack, but you have to be careful.*
↓
= Apply more pressure. Striking chance

ASSESSING THE LOCATION

PUSHING HIM BACK INTO OBSTACLES OR PILLARS. DON'T GIVE HIM A CHANCE TO GRASP HIS PREDICAMENT. IN ALL CASES, THE ENEMY IS FORCED INTO PLACES WITH BAD FOOTING OR WITH BARRIERS TO THE SIDES. AT ALL TIMES USE THE LOCATION'S FEATURES AND, ABOVE ALL, SEEK TO "WIN THE PLACE."

OUTSIDE	SUN TO YOUR BACK
INDOORS	ROOM AT YOUR SIDE, BACK, AND ABOVE…
NIGHT	FIRE AT YOUR BACK, SMALL KIAI…

ALWAYS TAKE THE HIGHER GROUND

MOVE YOUR ENEMY TO THE LEFT

GIVE YOURSELF PLENTY OF ROOM

3. Opponent doesn't change posture or sword = Opponent is primed to smash you if you carelessly go further. Read this and don't get fooled. Opponent will then have fleeting doubts.

↓

= Striking chance

Example 2. WINNING THE PLACE

1. Make sure that you are on the X, not the X.

↓

You control the centre of the court. Keeping opponent's back closest to the line puts pressure on opponent. The longer you are on the centre X, the more psychological advantage you have. Even when you aren't on the X, imagine that you are.

2. When the opponent has his back to the line and has planted his foot on the floor, move in closer and…

↓

Strike *men* from close in if their hands are lowered.

Strike *kote* from close in if their hands lift.

Strike *gyaku-dō* or *tsuki* from close in if they assume the three-point-defence posture.

Strike *kote-men* if the *maai* is a further out. (This will prevent him *oji-waza*'ing you, and will mean you will have enough balance to stay in the court, or even *taiatari* him out.)

If his back to the line, he will try to score with *debana-waza*…

If in *tsubazeriai*, he may try *hiki-waza*, even though he knows he will go out. Be careful.

3. When opponent is in the corner, and tries to escape in a circular motion…

↓

Cut him off with lateral movement. Don't use big steps. Small and fast. You can't strike when your left foot is off the ground, and you will be open.

Use your *shinai* to suppress the opponent's sword in the direction he is moving. He will move back or try to strike his way out.

If the opponent tries to make a big move back to the centre of court, *kaeshi-waza* is effective if he decides to attack.

Or, *debana-waza* if you time it when their left foot is off the ground when they are taking big steps.

If they try to come into *tsubazeriai*, they will relax for an instant when they arrive. *Hiki-waza* chance.

4. When YOU are trapped in the corner…

↓

Move diagonally forward in a circular motion, not laterally. Keep your *shinai* on the opponent's centreline while suppressing theirs.

If you move to the right, keep your *shinai* on the right side of their *shinai*, and on the left when moving to the left.

When you move to the right, they will usually target *men*…

When you move to the left, they will usually target *kote*…

If you opponent closes in, move forward while suppressing his *shinai*, pivot on contact, and *hiki-waza* back into the centre of court.

Eiga Naoki

Born 1967
Hokkaido
Policeman
Kyoshi 8-dan

2000 - 11th WKC Ind. Champ
2000 - 48th All Japan Champ
2003 - 12th WKC Team Champ
2019 - 17th 8-Dan Champion

PUBLICATIONS

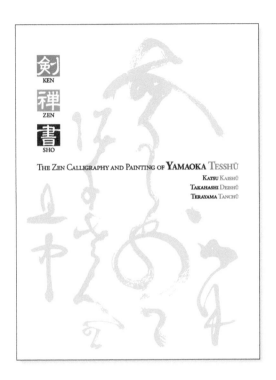

Ken Zen Sho

The Zen Calligraphy and Painting of Yamaoka Tesshu

Yamaoka Tesshu (1836-1888) was a Japanese master of the sword, Zen and calligraphy. This full-colour book on the Zen art of Yamaoka Tesshu features reproductions of extremely valuable calligraphy pieces, and also a number of essays about the relationship between swordsmanship, the study of Zen, and calligraphy. Each one of the works presented is translated into English, and its significance explained in detailed captions. Some fantastic specimens of Zen calligraphy by Tesshu's famous contemporaries Katsu Kaishu and Takahashi Deishu (Tesshu's brother-in-law), and modern master Terayama Tanchu are also featured.

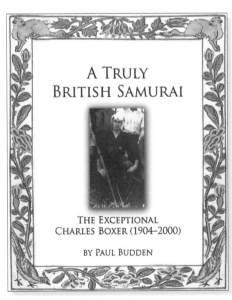

A Truly British Samurai
The Exceptional Charles Boxer

Budo Perspectives

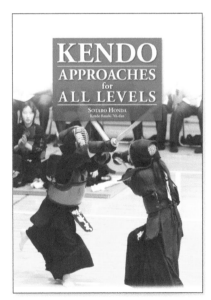

Kendo:
Approaches for all Levels

More info → www.kendo-world.com

Speed, Tension, Muscle type and Training

By James Ogle

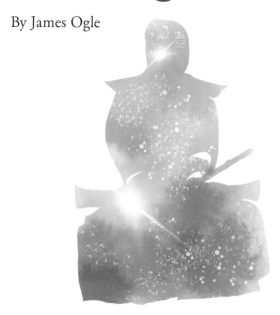

My job as a soft tissue therapist specialising in performance analysis has me dealing with athletes of all levels—from casual gym goers to international rugby teams, including the South African and Australian teams—with many different types of issue. In this article, I would like to address something that I regularly see (and experience!) in both my work and my kendo practice.

Something that occurs on a regular basis in my work are injuries or further technical issues caused by changes in technique/style. 80 % of the time this is the result of an individual trying to change their technique or action while carrying it out at the same speed/intensity that they were performing it at previously. What this tends to mean is that the wrong parts of the body are being used to develop the action. This is usually because they are tightening certain muscles in other areas of the body because they are not used to the new action, which consequently causes uneven stress to be put through the body, as well as making the movement/technique ineffective or damaging.

After conversations with multiple *sensei* (Hayashi Kozo-sensei (K8-dan), Honda Sotaro-sensei (K7-dan), Hiyama Yasuyuki-sensei (7-dan), Oda Yoshiko-sensei (R6-dan) and receiving information that was all very similar, I felt that these issues, which I was encountering with my patients at work, and the teaching I was receiving in my kendo were overlapping more and more.

In June 2017 we had a visit from Hayashi-sensei who talked about correct cutting and use of *tenouchi*. However, when he initially demonstrated and described the cutting action he talked about making each cut 100% and that they must be strong cuts. What followed for the next 30 minutes was everyone attending the seminar cutting as hard as they could and often injuring their training partners. Hayashi-sensei then took the time (with the help of Hiyama-sensei) to explain that he did not mean we had to hit hard, but that each cut should be sharp with the feeling of committing 100% to each cut, and that to achieve this you needed to relax and only use *tenouchi* to create a strong strike. I feel that this explanation fits in well with the science of biomechanics and developing movement patterns.

Developing the body to be able to produce a sharp movement means that you can attack in a smooth and quick action to be able to score *ippon*. To better understand how to do this, we need to understand the science behind the movements and how to maximise their effectiveness.

Broadly speaking there are two main types of muscle fibres: fast twitch and slow twitch. Most people are aware of this and the idea that fast twitch fibres are for moving quickly and slow twitch fibres are for endurance activities. This is not exactly true. Marathon runners train their slow twitch fibres and look at developing the muscles in the thighs, calves and upper body to resist fatigue, whereas sprinters will focus on explosive exercise such as sprint training and weight training to increase the oxygen flow to the muscle which allows them to increase the energy output for power production. But they are training areas of muscles that have a higher percentage of a certain type of fibre in those muscles already.

Here's how it works: Slow twitch fibres are the primary workers during aerobic exercises such as running or swimming. Once these fibres become tired, then and only then do the fast twitch fibres take over. We only start to recruit fast twitch fibres once we have reached a state of fatigue. (Crowther, G. J. and Gronka, R.K., 2003) So, the idea of "you must move quickly to train your fast twitch fibres" is no longer accurate. There is no conclusive evidence that you can transform your muscle fibres from slow to fast twitch, or vice-versa. (Wilson et.al., 2012) However, you also have two types of muscle groups involved in almost every action, the agonist (muscle causing the movement) and the antagonist (the muscle that must relax/stretch to allow the movement). This interaction of muscles has a much larger effect on the speed of movement, especially in kendo, than which type of muscle fibre you have more of.

So, we need to do repetitive *kihon* and push ourselves aerobically with movement and *kiai* to reach a level of fatigue so that we can use all of the muscle fibres in our movements (training hard), but we need to make sure we are activating the right muscles to allow the best movement so that the agonist is moving with its full range and the antagonist is relaxed and allowing this full range (working with the idea of "training smart"). We do not want a slow movement done repetitively; we want to develop a quick and sharp cut with a sharp body movement. But these two methods of training overlap and slower movements will benefit faster ones.

Due to the movements in kendo (and many other martial arts) being compound movements—movements that involve multiple parts of the body doing more than one simple action—we need to be able use the right muscles at the right time. The agonist needs to contract and the antagonist needs to relax/stretch to get the full movement. As an example, if you clench your fist and tense every muscle in your arm and then try to extend your

arm and wrist, it should be very difficult, if not impossible, to do, whereas if you relax the arm and extend it you will get a larger range of movement and it will be almost effortless.

This works for *suburi* as well. If you focus on cutting fast with the use of muscular power (using a movement which is not economical and relies on being bigger/physically stronger than the next person), you will end up actually reducing the speed of the movement as some of those muscle groups will need to complete multiple phases of relax/tighten/relax to allow the movement to take place. This often shows in the movement after a cut or in the *hasuji*, an obvious one being if the right arm is too tense the cut tends to come off to the side or is not sharp, and lacks sae as there is limited extension in the cutting action.

Most people do plenty of *kihon*, *waza*, *ji-geiko*, *shiai-geiko*, etc. and this is a proven way to improve our kendo.

However, how we use the body is equally as important. I am sure all of us have been told to relax by numerous *sensei* over the years, and a large part of this comes down to which muscles we are using and when. To develop a smooth and relaxed action at the shoulders for a large cut we need to have tone in the lower thoracic region of the spine to keep an upright posture while relaxing the muscles in the shoulder and neck, which will also help to drive us forward while allowing the shoulders full range of movement without restriction. To extend the wrists and use *tenouchi* when we strike, the posterior aspect of the forearm and triceps need to shorten while the biceps and deltoids relax to allow the arms to extend. To drive the body forward from the left leg we need to tighten and activate the gastrocnemius and soleus (calf muscles), the hamstrings and the glutes on the left side while the quads allow the movement of the hip and knee by extending.

The principle of relaxing to develop stronger or faster movement is no stranger to elite sports. If you watch Olympic sprinters as they run, the muscles in their legs (quadriceps, hamstrings, calves, hip flexors) are firing at full effect and driving them forwards, but their arms, though moving, are relaxed. You can see the muscle moving and bouncing back and forth as they run; the same with the muscles in their face (I am sure that we have all laughed at the funny lip and face movements of sprinters in the slow-motion replay when we were children!). This idea of using the muscles we require and keeping the other structures relaxed is something I believe would benefit many of us in our kendo practice. And it still isn't anything new there either.......

In his book *Kendo: Approaches for All Levels* (2012), Honda Sotaro states that kendo training should focus on developing movements through the process of:

1. big, slow and accurate
2. big, quick and accurate
3. small, quick and accurate

This process means that you train the body to use the correct muscles at the right time to develop the correct action. By doing this you only use the muscles required, whereas if you try to do an unfamiliar action quickly at the start, you will use more muscles than those required for the movement. As your training and level improves, then you can start to increase the speed of the movement. However, in kendo some aspects of training should always be kept at a slower pace in order to help to develop the action in a smooth and relaxed manner rather than using muscular power and becoming tense and making the technique incorrect. This movement can then be used in a quicker and sharper setting/application without the excess tension or strength.

Speaking to the *sensei* mentioned above, the conversation has always returned to using the body to develop a strong attack rather than using the arms to develop a quick or strong cut. We all know that a smooth relaxed movement is more effective and usually much quicker than being tense in our *keiko/shiai*, but the use of the body in the rest of our practice and actions tends to become less of a focus. Multiple *sensei* (including some of those above) have stressed that *suburi* is one of the most important aspects of kendo and is instrumental in developing a correct cutting action. Hiyama-sensei advocates *suburi* being done with a slow rhythm, not a slow cut as this should be sharp and crisp, but with a distinct time gap between each cut to help build a relaxed movement in the shoulders and develop a correct cutting action with a smooth movement. However, when it comes to *shiai* or applying your technique in a live situation, there is certainly a large element of speed.

Often the winners of competitions are fast, such as in the All Japan Kendo Championships over the last several years. However, the argument here is that they also have a variety of techniques at their disposal and know how and when to use them. This then comes into the area of training smart: to develop a variety of techniques at the individual's disposal, and staying relaxed so that the body and mind can respond smoothly and naturally to the situation. When watching these competitors, very rarely do they seem tense or like their range of movement is restricted or not smooth. Most of the time these individuals are able to move smoothly and attack from many different positions/angles due to their body being conditioned, but also relaxed so that they can activate the muscles and movements that they need when needed.

In terms of training and the process of progression, the ability to move at the right time and use the correct waza in the right situation, is due to practising for a long time, often a lifetime. Pushing the body at a young age to be able to produce speed and power; progressing to a more mature style of kendo and movement; and then into controlling their opponent so that they do not need to move quickly: this development is what allows us to continue practising and becoming better as we get older.

By starting at a young age, a focus can be placed purely on movement and speed as most children do not have the muscular power/conditioning to rely on strength, so they therefore develop a "light" and fairly relaxed movement. Particularly hard, physical kendo training in Japan is most often done during high school, usually after the individuals have developed a relaxed movement and can then add strength to their movements and attacks. For many of us our kendo career does not begin until we are in our late teens or twenties at the earliest, and Honda (2012) also mentions that training methods in the West need to be different than those in Japan, mainly due to the age difference and mixed abilities of classes, as well as the fact that just training as physically hard as possible probably is not the best method.

My belief is that most *kendoka* (especially those that tend to start at a later age or those that have a strong winning mentality) focus on cutting faster to be able to get *ippon* quicker and before their opponent. Being quick is not a bad thing, and Honda-sensei also says that a focus on speed tends to mean that the individual does not have control of the centre and only "hits" the target rather than cutting correctly. So, by focussing on relaxing, especially the neck, shoulders and arms, these individuals can develop a much better cutting action, a smoother attack that actually ends up faster, and reduces the risk of injury and increase the ability to score more *ippon*!

So, to maximise the effectiveness of our kendo practice and the time we spend doing it, we need to continually repeat *kihon* as it is the fundamental building block for everything else, but it must be

done with the correct action. To make sure we are doing this, an effective training method is to slow things down for certain parts of the training (suburi being a particularly good section to use) and focus on making a smooth and relaxed movement rather than a movement that is as fast as possible.

To summarise I will use a common phrase from coaching again:
Don't just train hard. Train smart.

References:
Crowther, G. J. and Gronka, R.K. "Fiber recruitment affects oxidative recovery measurements of human muscle in vivo", in *Medicine and Science in Sports and Exercise.* 2003, Mar.; 34(11).

Honda, S. *Kendo: Approaches for All Levels,* Bunkasha International Corporation, 2012.

Wilson, J.M., et al. "The effects of endurance, strength, and power training on muscle fiber type shifting", in *Journal of Strength and Conditioning Research.* 2012, June; 26(6): 1724-9.

All information in this article is from my own point of view/understanding, but I have tried to keep everything as close to the science underpinning it and to the information originally given to me. Any errors are my own.

A GUIDE TO JAPANESE ARMOUR

Text and Photos by Jo Anseeuw

Tetsu sabiji kikko-gane gata uchidashi go-mai-dō gusoku

There is a good reason why samurai armour, helmets, and masks only get a very brief and often rather dry description in museums, in most cases accompanied with the rather unhelpful Edo period time stamp: "1603-1868. Edo: A long and peaceful period in which armour slowly lost any practical use." The simple reason for this vagueness is because it is not always easy to date armour accurately, especially as it needed to be maintained over the years, with various parts needing to be replaced or upgraded to suit newer and more fanciful tastes. Researchers therefore hunt for pieces that are signed and, if possible, dated, (but this is very rare). Forgeries, both Edo period and more recent, also make the study of armour extremely difficult, especially if whole theories of the existence of certain smiths are based on one single item. Therefore, armour found together with or related to verifiable paperwork are treasures, as they often give clear hints about the owner, its price (as the paperwork is often a detailed order form) or the period of its manufacture. The set of armour presented in this article can actually be matched to documents from the Edo period and so can be verified with a high degree of certainty. It could be described as a *Tetsu sabiji kikko-gane gata uchidashi go-mai-dō gusoku* (armour with a breastplate made

> • **Name of Piece:**
> *Tetsu sabiji kikko-gane gata uchidashi go-mai-dō gusoku*
> (Armour with a breastplate made of five hinged sections with a russet iron finish. The hexagonal turtle-like pattern is embossed in the *dō*)
> 鉄錆地亀甲金形打出し五枚胴具足

of five hinged sections with a russet iron finish. The hexagonal turtle-like pattern is embossed in the *dō*), and it stands out for several reasons.

The *kabuto* (helmet) is of the *kawari* type, loosely translated as "spectacular helmet". During the Sengoku or Warring States period (1467-1603) in which many large-scale battles were fought, commanders distinguished themselves on the battlefields with often unique and spectacular helmets. Many of these helmets were based on a simple but very practical *zunari kabuto* (a helmet constructed using only three large plates) design, and enhanced with artistic structures in wood and lacquer. Also this particular helmet has a *zunari* shape base, and is covered with bear fur. Two horns give the *kabuto* an even stronger presence, while the brush *maedate* indicates that the owner may have had an artistic or literate side. If he had a sense of humour, it could be that he wanted to show his enemies he was going to write history with this battle.

The *menpō* (face guard), a *tetsu sabi ressei me no shita men*, has deeply forged features, and was used to protect the face during the battles. The actual usability of a *menpō* during battle is still greatly discussed in armour circles, but many agree that the *menpō* was very useful to allow a *kabuto* to be tied tightly under the chin. It is, however, likely that the removable nose was not used during an actual battle, to allow the wearer to breathe more freely and to shout commands to troops.

The *sangu* (term for the three armour components that protected the arms and legs) contains beautifully decorated *tetsu sabi shino-gote* (arm sleeves), *shu urushi nuri kozane haidate* to protect the thighs, and *tetsu sabi shino suneate* to protect the shins. The *suneate* contain finely etched diagonal *yasurime* lines, and *inome* motives. Such detail

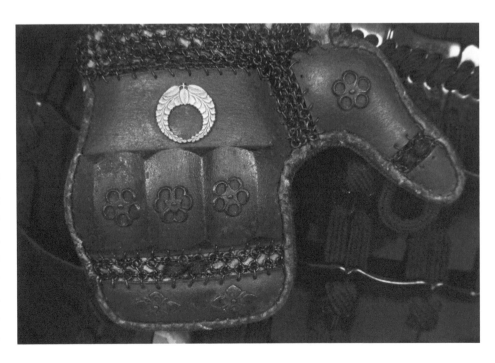

on smaller parts of the armour shows that it was not for a samurai of low rank. The fine butterfly shaped hinges near the top of the *kote*, combined with the orange-white lacing colour pattern that can be found all over the armour, show clearly the Kaga influence. The old Kaga province is located on the west coast of Japan, the southern part of present-day Ishikawa prefecture. The capital of Kaga was Kanazawa, which was ruled at a certain point in time by the Maeda clan. Kaga armour often has distinctive colours in their decorations (light green, orange, white, etc.), and also have certain features, like butterfly hinges, which are cloud like partition lines in the *dō*.

The most striking element of this armour is the beautiful *go-mai dō* (a *dō* consisting of five hinged sections). It consists of an embossed *kikko-gane gata* pattern of hexagonal shapes, and resembles a turtle. The Kaga style hinges also appear here, and the orange-white collar pattern in the lacing clearly shows that the set completely matches. The inside soft collar, reinforced with *kekko* plates beautifully trimmed with silk frills, again shows the high status of its owner.

What makes this armour historically interesting is the fact that the *dō* appears in the *Meikō zukan*. The *Meikō zukan* was written in the early 18th century by Munemasa Myōchin as a compendium of drawings of armour parts made by the famed Myōchin armour

鎧兜 A GUIDE TO JAPANESE ARMOUR

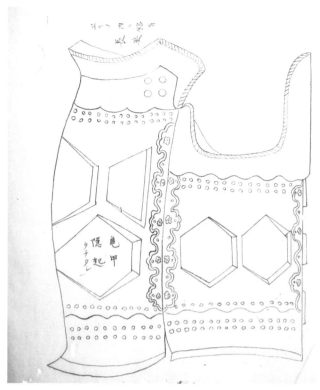

Partial front and side view of the dō *as illustrated in the* Meikō zukan

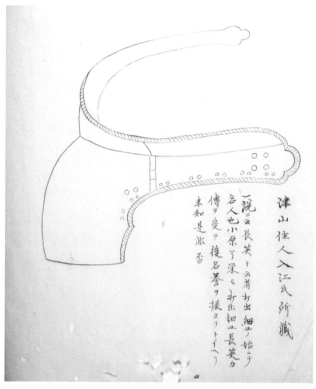

Part of the collar and shoulder strap of the dō *as illustrated in the* Meikō zukan

Back view of the dō *as illustrated in the* Meikō zukan

family. However, this is also a family that was famous for rewriting its own history, a fact that continues to confuse many armour collectors today.

Matsumiya Kanzan (1686-1780), a strategist and probably the best armour connoisseur of his time, was asked to write a preface to the *Meikō zukan* in 1736. Luckily, Matsumiya wrote his own follow-up work with drawings that he was able to make all over Japan. That work, also dedicated to the Myōchin school, is called the *Meikō zukan zokushū*, with an appendix related to other schools called *Meikō zukan fukan*. These were probably completed in 1746. An addendum, devoted exclusively to the works of Ryōei and Fukushima Kunitaka, was probably published posthumously. About 22 partial and three complete copies (mostly copies of copies) survive today. The work done by Matsumiya is extremely important as he did not follow official Myōchin doctrine, but added annotations and technical details to the drawings that were based on real pieces he could actually put his hands on. It is in the *Meikō zukan zokushū* section of the *Meikō zukan* that this *dō* appears. This therefore means that the *dō* dates to earlier than 1746. In the notes written by Matsumiya, we learn that the *dō* was made by a certain Chōei, but it is not clear if Chōei is the student of Ohara Ryōei, as the manuscript claims, or vice versa.

For more information about the *Meikō zukan*, Robert Burawoy has completed a PhD thesis about the subject, and has recently published a new version of his marvellous book (in French), *Etude du Meikō Zukan - Armuriers du Japon XVIe-XVIIIe siècle* (Institut des Hautes Etudes Japonaises - Collège de France: Editions De Boccard, 2017).

***

Jo Anseeuw is a director the Nihon Katchū Bugu Kenkyū Hozon-kai (NKBKHK - Association for the Research and Preservation of Japanese Helmets and Armor). In April 2017, a Western Branch of the NKBKHK was established: The Japanese Armor Society, with the aim of making knowledge about Japanese armor more accessible in English. More information about the society's activities can be found on their homepage: http://japanese-armor.org/eng/

鎧 兜 A GUIDE TO JAPANESE ARMOUR

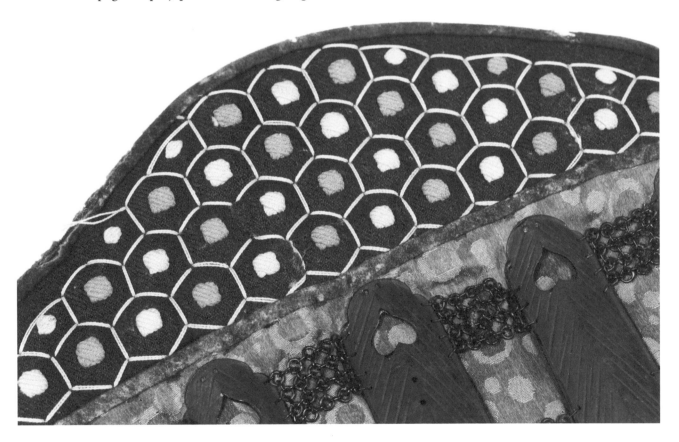

PASSING 7TH DAN
REFLECTIONS—FEELINGS—MEANING

by Gabriel Weitzner

November 28, 2017, was a nice sunny, blue-sky morning in Shinagawa, Japan. Everything was prepared the night before: *bōgu*, new *men-himo*, *hakama*, *keiko-gi*, etc. After breakfast, I hopped on the train to get to the Tokyo Budokan to challenge for the 7-dan examination for the second time in Japan.

During the train ride, I had plenty of opportunity to reminisce on my journey thus far. I previously challenged twice without success in Canada. During a conversation with Taro Ariga-sensei, who I have known for a very long time, he said, "Hey Gabriel, why you don't challenge in Japan? For your age group, you will do fine." I don't know about you, but when somebody says to you, "for your age, you are OK", it is not exactly a great feeling. However, as we are old, close friends, I figured I'd better listen.

The first time, I applied for the 7-dan grading convened in May just before the Kyoto Taikai and received authorization from the Canadian Kendo Federation with plenty of support from Christian D'Orangeville-sensei.

I arrived at the Kyoto Arena and went to my examination area. My first impression when I checked my name on the list and looked around at everybody in my group was "OMG do I really look that old?" I then understood the meaning of Taro's words. Everybody was friendly. I was the only non-Japanese, so everybody went out of their way to make me feel welcome. Hamaguchi-sensei, and kendo folks from his dojo came to wish me success. I kind of felt at home, but I didn't pass this time. Failure is a great teacher. It provides the best advice if you are open to it. Failure is a bitter pill but is something that must be embraced. I didn't pass, but I had a very strong feeling that I was on the correct path. "But, what is missing?" I asked myself.

A saying came to mind that has stuck with me: "If you want to get something you never had before, you have to be willing to do something you never did before." I realised that "something" was my "kendo mind". In needed to create a powerful image of my understanding of kendo in my own mind. I had to believe…

I am not sure if you realise this, but *Kendo World* has published over the years an unbelievable amount of very valuable information by countless clever kendo folks. Articles like, "Hanshi Says…" and "Breathing", as well as articles on such topics as the Nippon Kendo Kata, grading, and so much more. You really should spend time on going over all the old editions of *Kendo World*. [Ed. Note: Thank you for the plug!] Some of the articles are very inspiring, like "Passing 7-Dan: Reflections after the Facts" by Donatella

Castelli-sensei, and "Making the Grade" by Roberto Kishikawa-sensei after passing the 8-dan examination. In short, I started to work my kendo mind.

I also had conversations with Kishikawa-sensei, who I have known for many years; exchanged thoughts with Geoff Salmon-sensei from the U.K.; and, had several conversations with Taro Ariga-sensei, who is now in California. In Japan, I got together with Itoh-sensei in Tokyo, Hamaguchi-sensei in Osaka, and Sumi-sensei in Fukuoka. I went over my notes of previous conversations with Murayama-sensei, Onuma-sensei, Toda-sensei, and Chiba-sensei, all great kenshi who have since passed away. Fukumoto-sensei told me once: "You have to think that 7-dan is not the grade that comes after 6-dan, but it is the grade that comes before 8-dan." I have never forgot that powerful yet simple advice.

I acquired and read as much information as I could get my hands on. In the end, one thing stuck with me: I must show the examiners something special, personal, different, and unique about myself. I have to show them the beauty of my kendo. Put it this way, you only have two minutes to face each opponent whom you know nothing about. Against these unknowns, you have to perform at the top of your ability. I thought I was facing an blank canvas, and had to be ready to write a beautiful kanji on it. The beauty expressed on that canvas will determine if I passed or not.

The biggest challenge in the arena for me was to keep calm and focussed during the seven-plus hours of waiting. My motivation was to express the creativity and beauty of my kendo. It seems that I accomplished my objective. Not because I succeeded, but because I do not remember what I did. I do recall the sound of my *shinai* hitting the target, but nothing else. Does this mean I was in a state of complete *mushin*?

We did not have to wait a long time for the results as we were the last few hundred left at Tokyo Budokan. There were about 4,000 people challenging that day, but only 174 passed, and I was the only non-Japanese to do so.

When I was waiting for the official result to be posted, I had a good feeling that everything went well. But actually seeing my number—216 A—on the board was a phenomenal sensation. I will never forget it as long as I live.

The first thing that popped into my mind was my late wife Silvia. The exam took place at a very special time. That week was the anniversary of her passing. It was because of her support that I was able to travel to the Kitamoto Seminar many times, visit different universities and kendo dojo, to go to *asa-geiko* at Keishichō Police Dojo, journey to Kyoto and Fukuoka for training… I am extremely grateful to her.

The next moment, I had to get ready for the Nippon Kendo Kata portion of the exam. There was not much time to regroup as partners were picked in less than 3 minutes. I had to listen to the instructions in Japanese and prepare myself mentally. Luckily my partner, 216 B, was also my opponent in my first bout. When that part of the exam was over, a tremendous feeling of gratitude embraced me once more.

On the Yamanote Line train to Shinagawa many things raced through my head: *keiko* with the late Miyagui-sensei at Nihon-Jin Kai in Buenos Aires, Argentina; *kakari-geiko* with the late Murayama-sensei in Fukuoka; advice from the late Toda-sensei and from Itoh-sensei in Tokyo; conversations with Hamaguchi-sensei in Osaka; the list goes on. Back at the hotel I sent an email to everybody who supported me with "Canada has a new 7-dan" plastered in the subject line. I was proud of that title. I was exhausted but could not sleep, so went to soak in a hot bath. Just when I was ready to sleep, the phone rang. It was my kendo brother, Yamada-san, calling from Thailand to congratulate me. We talked for a very long time.

It took several days for my accomplishment to sink in, followed by the realization that I now have a huge weight of responsibility on my shoulders. I still have to keep acknowledging my kendo shortcomings with a humble and open mind to fix them. In that sense, nothing at all has changed. Kendo is certainly a path that never ends.

An Exploration of How to Correct the Bad Habit Among Kendo Practitioners of 'Chin-raising' when Striking

Takenaka Kentaro
  (National Institute of Fitness and Sports in Kanoya)
Shimokawa Mika
  (National Institute of Fitness and Sports in Kanoya)

Refereed

Keywords: Chin, Field of Vision, Monomi

Overview

This research investigates how to correct the habit of chin-raising when executing *men* strikes. Raising the chin can be dangerous when receiving the opponent's *tsuki-waza* (thrust to the throat) and can negatively impact stability and striking power. Improvement here will conceivably lead to both increased safety and striking ability.

We refined a special method to mitigate the problem and ascertained its effectiveness in *kendoka* who habitually raise their chins when striking. Through blocking the field of vision below the *monomi* on the *mengane* we were able to impede the tendency to rely on lower visual information when striking. The results of our experiments proved this to be an effective method for remedying "chin-raising".

I. Introduction

In the traditional Japanese martial art of kendo, importance is placed on adhering to the basics and learning "correct techniques" (*waza*). With numerous competitions, however, many practitioners show tendencies of being more concerned with winning at all costs to the detriment of acquiring correct *waza* (AJKF, 2010). If a *kendoka* develops bad habits in their quest to win competitions, these are not easily remedied later. If he or she then becomes a teacher, it will be difficult to provide students with a model for appropriate striking movement.

This study focuses on the striking action of a university-level *kendoka* who consistently raises his chin when striking. This is not only a safety concern against an opponent's *tsuki-waza*, but also adversely affects suitable posture and strength necessary to complete a valid strike.

Earlier research looking at this problem (Kizuka, 2010) confirms, "When the head inclines back and the arms are extended, physiologically speaking this is a 'tonic neck reflex'. In order to quickly extend the arms, the front part of the neck should be free of unnecessary force. As the body moves forward rapidly, the head may follow making the chin raise." It must also be pointed out that, "Copying the form of raising the chin when striking *men* is not only erroneous, but will make the habit ingrained."

Furthermore, Kidera et al (2006) states: "If the chin is pulled in, muscles on the collarbone contract, mobility of the shoulder blades is hindered, and movement of the arms becomes restricted." Retracting the chin in the *kamae* causes "posture to collapse and the striking action to become hampered at the moment of striking." Therefore, it is imperative that "chin-raising" be rectified during the striking action, not before.

We were able to verify that it is fixable through a special method of *keiko* whereby the participant's field of vision is circumscribed.

II. Research Method and Case Study

1. Case Study

The subject of this study (Player A) is a 19-year-old male (height: 168 cm; weight: 61 kg). He has approximately 13 years of kendo experience from the first-grade of elementary school through to the first year of university. His main competitive achievement is reaching second place at the All Japan High School Kendo Tournament.

2. Correction Methodology for "Chin-raising"

Player A exhibited a tendency to raise his chin when striking. To correct his movement, we temporarily restricted his field of vision below the *monomi* of the *mengane*. The *monomi* is the gap in the *mengane* (metal bars on the front of the *men*) directly in front of the eyes, usually between the sixth and seventh bars from the top of the *men*. We used a specially-made cloth (Fig. 1) affixed to the *men* to obstruct Player A's vision from the *monomi* down (Fig. 2). In other words, the more his chin was raised, the less he could

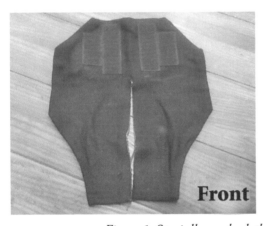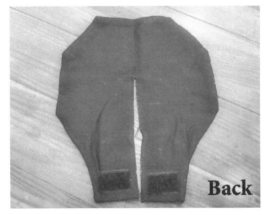

Figure 1. Specially-made cloth for restricting the field of vision.

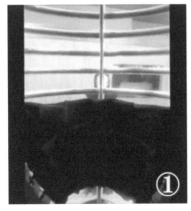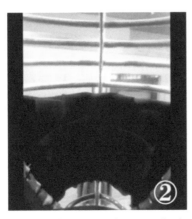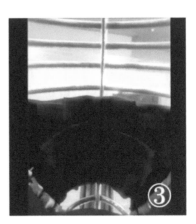

Figure 2. Field of vision from inside the **men**.

see, and the less visual information he received about his opponent (Fig. 2. ①–③)

3. Correction Period and Training

The correction period lasted approximately five weeks, from October 29 to December 5, 2013. Player A's schedule included six training sessions per week after classes (two hours per practice), as well as 50-minutes morning practice twice a week. Player A practised with a limited field of vision during all training sessions for the duration of the study, which was conducted during the competitive off-season. The morning practices consisted of 25-minutes of *kiri-kaeshi*, and 25-minutes of *uchikomi* training. The after-school training sessions consisted of basic practice (*kirikaeshi*, *uchikomi*, and *kakari-geiko*) for 60-minutes, followed by 50-minutes of *jigeiko* (*gokaku-geiko*, sparring). For this entire period, Player A had his vision restricted in the manner described above meaning that he could not see his opponent if he raised his chin.

4. Evaluating the Effectiveness of the Correction Method

To evaluate changes in Player A's "chin-raising" when striking, we captured still photos from video taken during training and matches when he was striking *men*. We compared and analysed the degree of "chin-raising" exhibited before and after the correction period.

To assess the effectiveness of the correction methodology, we also interviewed Player A about other methods he had tried and previous instruction he had received with regard to his habit of "chin-raising".

III. Results

1. Striking Motion of Player A During Training with a Restricted Field of View

In this study, we observed Player A's movements as he underwent a correction period training with blocked visual cues. After the cloth was attached to the *mengane*, Player A was able to improve his striking motion by not raising his chin. This improvement was not gradual; it happened immediately from the time visibility was restricted. Player A never lifted his

Figure 3. Player A's men *strike before his field of vision was restricted.*

chin during *uchikomi* and *kirikaeshi*, and also during *gokaku-geiko*.

2. Using Photographs to Ascertain Improvement

(1) Before Implementation

Figure 3 shows Player A striking *men* during an actual practice session with no restrictions to his field of

Figure 4. Player A's men strike after his field of vision was restricted.

vision. From the lead-up (Fig. 3–②) to the moment of the strike (Fig. 3–③) we can observe a backward inclination of the head. The chin clearly rises at the time of the strike, and despite the forward inclination of the upper body from the neck down, the head is tilting backward. We can also see that the posture is broken at the moment of striking.

(2) Striking Motion after Training with Limited Visibility

Following the correction period, we removed the cloth from Player A's *mengane* and examined his technique. In the photographs of his *men* strike (Fig. 4) there is little evident backward inclination of the head from the lead-up (Fig. 4–②) to the moment of impact (Fig. 4–③). Furthermore, his posture from the head down to the waist was also stable. There was still a slight tendency to kick the left foot back with the sole is visible (Figure 3–③), but the subject still shows improvement.

3. Post-experiment Interviews (Player A)

We conducted interviews with Player A about past kendo training, the background of his "chin-raising" habit, advice received from instructors, and the kind of efforts he made to improve. The following information was collected.

(1) How the Habit Developed

In elementary school, Player A tried to increase the speed of his strike. He developed a tendency to raise his chin as a result of his efforts to move faster. He understood the need to fix this problem, and even though he consciously attempted to make improvements during practice, he was unsuccessful.

(2) Instructions Regarding "Chin-raising"

Instructors started pointing out the problem to him from the sixth grade of elementary school. From that time, he was reprimanded constantly, particularly in sixth grade, in the third year of middle school, and in the second year of high school. He received the same advice from different teachers.

(3) Improvement Methods Attempted

Player A tried not raising his chin. As an example of a specific method he used to fix the problem, he tried practising with a stick tied to his back in the second year of middle school. He placed a *bokutō* in the *koshi-ita* of his *hakama* and tied it to his *men-himo* to stop his head tilting backwards as he struck, but improvement was negligible. The subject also felt that his striking action had become rigid as a result.

IV. Discussion

1. Improvement through Visibility Restriction

As confirmed through photographs, a notable difference could be observed before and after the application of visibility restriction. "Chin-raising" when striking *men* was significantly reduced. In normal circumstances, it is possible to see the opponent through bars in the *mengane* other than the *monomi*. Restricting vision below the *monomi* makes it impossible to have a clear view when the chin is raised. Therefore, the habit was largely fixed over the training period where his vision was limited to seeing through the *monomi*. Consequently, Player A's *men* strike was also judged to have improved as a result.

An important kendo teaching is "*Ichigan-nisoku-santan-shiriki*" (First, the eyes; second, the feet; third, a strong mind; fourth, power). This means that it is essential for practitioners to have an uninterrupted visual bearing on their opponent, and this should be a priority when training. This study has shown that remedying "chin-raising" in this way augments an immediate improvement in skill.

2. Improvement Method Validity

Player A declared that he was unable to rectify this problem during his junior high school days by using a *bokutō* fixed to his back to restrict movement and promote correct striking posture. Another method was needed. Player A also stated that his previous attempts to improve made it harder for him to move, suggesting that it had a harmful effect on the upper body. Other bad habits could also conceivably result from this, and cause physical harm to the practitioner.

No physical burden was placed on the subject in this experiment. Furthermore, the subject did not need to modify body movement. Thus, it is plausible that this method is an effective way of improving kendo in people of all ages who have difficulty comprehending what correct kendo posture is supposed to be. In other words, not limited to the habit of "chin-raising", such means could effectively improve overall kendo posture, prevent unnecessary vertical movement, and correct the positioning of the left foot. Thus, our findings suggest that this form of practice is a valid means for technical improvement and warrants further consideration.

V. Summary

This research investigated the idea that restricting vision would prevent chin-raising in a kendo strike. Actual testing showed considerable improvement in the chin position when striking. Until the experiemnt, Player A habitually obtained visual information from underneath the *monomi* when striking. Blocking the field of view under the *monomi* forced Player A to look through the *monomi* leading to immediate improvement. There is no guarantee that the chin-lifting habit will not return when the field of view under the *monomi* is unobstructed, so we can only surmise that the fix is temporary.

Chin-raising during the strike is not only seen in athletes like Player A who are seeking to better their performance in competition, but also in young children who have not developed enough physical strength, and also in elderly practitioners who have gone through a decline in muscular power. Especially with younger kendo players, continual admonishment for lifting their chin may lead to decreased motivation to train.

In our research, we used a specially designed cloth to restrict the view under the *monomi*, but tape would achieve the same results. We hope that our findings will assist kendo practitioners in Japan and around the world.

VI. References

1) Ichikawa Hajime, Takayama Kotaro (2008), *Ima tsutaetai kendo shugyo no kokoro-e,* Ski Journal, p. 10
2) Kizuka Tomohiro (2010), *Chikara wo nuku,* Ski Journal, pp. 30-31
3) Kidera Hidefumi, Oda Shingo (2006), *Kenshi nara shitte okitai 'karada' no koto,* Taishuukan Shoten, pp. 10-11, 50-52
4) MEXT, "Nenrei-betsu taikaku sokutei no kekka", http://www.e-stat.go.jp/SG1/estat/List. do?bid=000001050841&cycode=0
5) Takano Sasaburo (1991 reprinted), *Kendo kyohon,* Shimazu Shobo, p. 55
6) AJKF (2010), *Kendo shido yoro,* p. 9

SHINAI SAGAS
I See You

By Charlie Kondek
Artwork by Phillip Solomon

In all the years I've been involved in kendo, among the dozens of people whose experiences I have come to know well, I cannot think of anyone that had a plan for their kendo when they began. Certainly I have known people, primarily Japanese, who pledged at the outset a lifelong commitment to the art. And surely there must be some people out there who visualised themselves becoming a champion or an accomplished master from the beginning, though I don't know anyone like that personally. What is more common, in my experience, is that we are drawn to kendo, to its aesthetics and traditions, its rigour and action, without any realistic expectation of what kendo will do for us. We discover afterward and over long periods of time the kind of kendoka we are or can be.

I think about this when I think about my own kendo, but especially when I think about the kendo of someone like Jake Patric. I don't remember the day Jake started practising at our dojo as a boy; I only remember becoming cognizant of the effort conveyed by his quiet, earnest, freckled face and its place in the line-up of kenshi practising *suburi* and *waza*. I remember him practising in shorts and dirty t-shirts, then in *hakama* and *keikogi*; I remember when he, like so many other kids that stuck with it, was allowed to wear *bōgu*, in stages, first with *tare* and *kote*, then *dō*, then *men*. And I remember not being surprised when Jake began to do well in competitions. After all, he was always so serious in *keiko* and displayed such great effort. And honestly, in our region, it was expected that a hard worker like Jake would do well in the youth division, which had some real rockets in it but also a lot of cautious fencers that hadn't yet developed confidence and courage in their attacks. Anyone with good skill and fast *men* cut was a strong contender at this level; doubly so if that person could also bring to bear a good small *kote*. I envied kids like Jake. I wished I had started kendo as a kid and not as an adult, although there is nothing to say I would have had Jake's discipline at that age.

Even before he'd gotten into his *bōgu*, Jake must have come into contact with old Gower. Rod Gower was a fixture at our dojo, and I could not remember a time when he hadn't been. Like me, and unlike Jake, Gower had started kendo as an adult. Unlike me, unlike Jake, I could not picture Gower as anything but a pale, uninspiring lump of middle-aged man; that he had ever been a vigorous, skybound youth was unimaginable, and attempts to envision him thus succeeded only in transporting to the head and shoulders of a boy, Rod's thin, black hair, which tufted above the ears, black plastic spectacles, and lip-concealing black moustache. To say that Gower had started kendo "as an adult" was to learn that Gower had been an awkward white-collar budo enthusiast as far back as the 1980s, when he had migrated from karate—a fitting setting for his moustache and computer-clerk looks—to what was then in our part of North America a fledgling kendo scene. In all that time, Gower had attained, after several tries at each level, the rank of 2-dan, and for some time had been eyeing the 3-dan exam. He was an excellent source of lore for the kendo in our area, but you had to be careful how you accessed this data, as Rod would be only too happy to talk the topic past exhaustion.

This was actually true of a lot of topics for Gower, and I sometimes wondered if his wife and teenage kids were grateful that kendo got the man out of the house so consistently. Gower was free and prolific with kendo advice, which he was especially wont to dispense in the sweaty yellow haze that hung in the dojo after *keiko* as a dozen or two dozen people retired their drenched *bōgu* and battered *shinai*. This was usually a time of happy, weary talk, and Gower, who had worked as hard if not as well as the rest of us, contributed his voice to a fairly congruent din. And it must be noted that the advice Gower gave was never incorrect or that his opinion was

outlandish, only that he could deliver his remarks with authority but not actuality. He might, for example, give someone pointers for executing *maki-waza*; at his best, he would cite the videos he had watched about it, the articles he'd read, the sensei whose instruction he was repeating; he couldn't perform the *waza* very well himself.

That's the way it was with Gower—well intended but long winded and without the particular credence that comes from experience. I imagine there are guys like him in every gym and every sportsman's discipline all over the world. Most people tolerated him—some, I'm sure, despised him—but he was easy to tolerate, since the annoying aspects of his personality were offset by the good humour, gentle intentions, and the overall camaraderie of the dojo. He might over-stay his welcome in a conversation, but he never forced himself on anyone. But when I say Jake Patric must certainly have encountered Gower when he became a regular in our club, this is what I mean, that soon Jake would have had the same encounters with Gower we all had. Indeed, they would have been systematic encounters, since Gower tended to lecture or give "extra pointers" to the beginners on fundamentals, on the care and acquisition of equipment, and the attitude of *reigi* in the dojo and to the sensei.

I cannot put my finger on when Jake became an adult, or whatever it is we now call people in their early 20s. And I cannot recall when Jake's talent in kendo beyond seriousness and hard work became evident. *Ji-geiko* with him afforded harsh awakenings to the potency of his ability; at some point he was old enough that I didn't have to hold back on him while sparring, and then I found myself having to work harder to dominate the fight; then, I was unable to dominate it at all, and was working just to keep up. He'd developed that *men* cut that some people have that comes at you in the flick of an eyelash and is like stepping into oncoming traffic. And his *kote*—bullwhip sharp and bone rattling—he seemed to be able to place just by pointing an index finger. I wasn't the only one that noticed, and *ji-geiko* wasn't the only opportunity to observe his prowess; he became a frequent recipient of medals at the annual competitions, where he now competed at the adult level. He passed his *shinsa* easily, it seemed, and was soon a 2-dan. People spoke of him as a natural candidate for our federation's national team some day.

This kind of transformation in a kenshi not only affects his individual trajectory but his gravitational pull. We had always liked Jake, but now many of us admired him, and especially among people his age and younger, he was emulated and looked to for leadership. He took to this as quietly and seriously as everything else, always patiently concentrating on the task at hand, and with the appropriate degree of participation. Unlike our friend Gower, Jake was reluctant and cautious with advice, not out of stinginess but in apparent, humble acknowledgment of the fact that, after all, he was not one of the teachers, and still a young man finding his way. The most he would offer were explanations like, "Well, the way I think of it is…" or "Something that has helped me is…"

Just as I am unable to discern the exact moments that Jake pivoted from child to man, so, too, am I unable to note exactly when Jake and Gower had become friends. I think now it must have happened in Jake's boyhood when, among the kids captured in one of Gower's verbose dragnets, Jake looked on the old man with appreciation and a respectful absorption of Gower's words was signalled by his young face, the bright beam of which remained fixed on Gower's fluttering black moustache while the fidgety attention of others wandered. I remember now a time when Gower's car broke down. I remember Jake asking the general assembly, "Where's Rod-sempai?" And I remember for a time Jake picking Gower up in his own car, and their simultaneous arrival at the dojo, Gower continuing some point he had made on the drive, expanded in the parking lot, further digressed as the two carried their *bōgu* and *shinai* to a corner of the gym. Too, Jake would encourage the young peers that pressed him for ideas or advice to seek the counsel of Gower. "Ask Gower-san about that; he has some good ideas." This was especially acute when the topic of budo history or context was raised, or the looking after of equipment, or the foundational elements of footwork, *kamae*, and cut.

Yes, this was a remarkable friendship, one that earned a puzzled frown from some of the other kenshi.

Jake Patric, they seemed to ask with their rumpled eyebrows, was an emergent Henry, so why did he cling to his relationship with the local Falstaff? As I watched Jake Patric watching Rod Gower, I began to see Gower with Jake's eyes, or maybe with some filter of Jake's that had been placed over my own eyes. When I considered Jake Patric compared to Rod Gower, I saw a young man whose body through the coaxing of *keiko* bent to the inhabitant's desire. Jake had only to will his sword to move and it moved, and his feet and abdomen followed. Gower's body seemed in constant rebellion. If he hurried, his actions fell apart, and so was an instrument better played slowly and deliberately. It was not just their difference in age, it was a difference of talent, of aptitude. Jake could expect a return on his investment of hard work. Gower put in the same work, and yielded not nearly the dividends.

Perhaps that was the key to the whole thing. Perhaps that's what Jake saw in Gower that so few of us appreciated. And in that way, perhaps Jake—quiet, serious Jake—anticipated what so few of us anticipated and what had not even blemished him: the biting, iron frost of age, the rust that inhibits the ponderous, thumping machinery. Perhaps Jake recognized Gower's struggles to achieve, which is, frankly, amazing when one considers Jake's own achievements, in a shorter amount of time, and the lofty perspective it afforded him. Unblinded by medallions of bronze and silver, with his eye on gold, Jake Patric from his high climb looked back to see how Rod Gower laboured toward the same summit.

Looked back, and reached back. I said earlier that Gower was "eyeing" the 3-dan exam. It would be more accurate to say Rod has attempted it a few times, and not yet succeeded. As of this writing, Rod Gower and Jake Patric are training for that exam together. You can see them at *keiko*, bantering before practice starts, and in the rotation of partners hear Jake's encouraging shouts and Gower's enthusiastic reply; and when we have *gōdō-geiko*, Jake and Rod are often together, sparring apart from everyone else, pausing to make note of something and trade ideas, then resuming the fight. No one at our dojo doubts Jake Patric can pass this exam. Few of us sense the feat of endurance it is for Rod to keep pursuing it.

Inishie wo Kangaeru

By Alex Bennett

A look at some of the old teachings in kendo

Miyamoto Musashi (1582–1645) is a name that all *kenshi* have heard of. Arguably the most famous Japanese swordsman of all time, the truth is that much of what we know about his life is shrouded in mystery. Even when he was alive, conspiracy theories and misconceptions about the man were the norm, and his legend has never stopped growing. Although writings on Musashi over the centuries is a mishmash of fact and fiction, one thing that cannot be denied is the profound influence his teachings have had on the philosophical underpinnings of modern kendo. His magnum opus, *Gorin-no-sho* (1645) is a veritable treasure trove of wisdom for *kenshi*. Although some of his principles seem abstract or irrelevant in the context of the modern sport of kendo, peeling back the layers of the text will reveal timeless and universal truths that extend far beyond the dominion of swordsmanship. In fact, *Gorin-no-sho* can surely be considered a ground-breaking primer into what we know now as sports psychology.

Of the multitude of instructions Musashi passes on to his students, one that intrigues me more than ever of late regards "gaze". Many readers may have heard the old Musashi saying "Look at a far mountain". In a section titled "About the Gaze in Strategy", Musashi explains the following:

Miyamoto Musashi
(1582–1645)

"One's gaze should be expansive and far-reaching. This is the dual gaze of 'looking in' (*kan*) and "looking at" (*ken*). The gaze for 'looking in' is intense whereas that for 'looking at' is gentle. It is of utmost importance for a warrior to see distant things as if they were close and close things as if they were distant."

He advises that the "warrior must know the enemy's sword without even seeing it." In other words, the swordsman must NOT focus his attention only on the opponent's weapon, hands, face, feet, or any other specific point. Focusing only on minute details will make you forget "bigger issues" he warns, and your mind will become confused meaning that certain victory will slip from your reach. Instead, he must take in all of it.

I am reminded of legendary basketball players like Magic Johnson and Larry Bird who were able to make stunning "no-look" or "blind" rocket-paced passes to teammates in feats of almost supernatural awesomeness. Is this related to what Musashi meant by "see distant things as if they were close and close things as if they were distant"? Sort of. Clearly you might be looking in one direction, but you are completely aware of what is happening around you, where your opponents (and/or allies) are and their speed, cadence, and distance, *etc*. Such situational awareness can only be nurtured through years of dedicated training and extends beyond matters of mere technical skill. It is all very much in the mind.

In the final scroll of *Gorin-no-sho*, "Ether", Musashi further states that the warrior must polish the two layers of his mind, the "heart of perception" and the "heart of intent", and sharpen his two powers of observation, *kan* ("looking in") and *ken* ("looking at"). It is important to remember here that the interaction is a two-way street, and to be aware that a skilled opponent will be "looking at" and "looking in" to his mind as well. Knowing this means that you can take control of what your opponent sees and perceives. As he observes your movements and penetrates the inner reaches of your mind (or so he thinks) make him feel at home. To achieve this is to be in control of your opponent but requires that you have absolute faith in your intuitive powers. That is,

the swordsman must have the capacity to listen to gut feelings instead of reacting only to what can be seen externally.

According to Harteis and Billett (2013), intuition is defined as "the capability to act or decide appropriately without deliberately and consciously balancing alternatives, and without following a certain rule or routine, and, possibly, without awareness". In simple terms, this is essentially reading the opponent's mind. In sports science the modern term for this concept is referred to as "empathic accuracy". Such an ability is not magical. Quite simply, it is a very advanced communicative capability to sense what your opponent is feeling or thinking by interpreting basic body language cues such as their eyes, face colour, countenance, cadence, respiratory patterns, physical tautness, voice tone, and being in the moment. Because you see close things as if they were far away, and far away things as if they were close, you perceive your environment as a whole, and can hear your intuition loud and clear.

In so many ways, the culmination of Musashi's "Way of combat strategy" is an unconditional belief in the self, and subsequently an unwavering conviction to act according to your intuition. This in turn points to the ultimate realm in swordsmanship, and everything for that matter. Musashi calls this the Ether (also referred to as the Void). The Ether is not Nirvana or enlightenment in the Buddhist sense: it is to break through the clouds of confusion and see all things with unimpeded clarity.

There is Good, not Evil in the Ether
There is Wisdom
There is Reason
There is the Way
The Mind, Empty

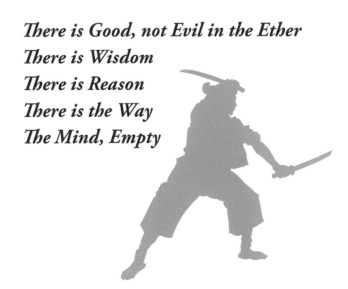

H8-dan Sumi Masatake-sensei's Visit to Cordoba, Argentina
By Gabriel Weitzner

"First of all, we must keep in mind our own history, our origins and what we have learned until now from many sensei. Who you are now, represents your collective Kendo experience, and all the people you have met. We have countless influences during our kendo journey."
— Roberto Kishikawa-sensei

In 1984, I went for the very first time to the Foreign Kendo Leaders Summer Seminar in Kitamoto. At that time this *gasshuku* was a gruelling two weeks long. Instructors at that camp were Murayama-sensei, Toda-sensei, Sugu-sensei, Kobayashi-sensei, Ota-sensei, and Shioiri-sensei. I shared that time with fellow kenshi like Graham Sayer, Gerhard Tscherter, Paul Budden, and Sue Lytollis. We still see each other today.

In the early 1990s, I attended Paul Budden's Kodokan Dojo Seminar. I had the privilege of meeting Sumi Masatake-sensei, and over the years we have met several times in Japan. At the last Kyoto Embu Taikai in 2017, Sumi-sensei and I chatted over dinner about his experiences around Europe, and we discussed the possibility of introducing him to Argentina's wine and *asado* (barbecued meat) culture.

Kendo Cordoba—Butokuden Dojo Gustavo Adolfo Ramos

Occupying most of the Southern portion of South America, Argentina extends 3460 km (2150 miles) from the northern tip of the country to Tierra del Fuego, the most southern place. Cordoba is situated just in the middle north of the country, and it is home to the Butokuden Dojo.

Over the years, many kendoka have visited Butokuden Dojo: Fukumoto-sensei from Japan; Taro Ariga-sensei, at that time from Canada; Pauline Stolarz-sensei from France; Asuncion Gonzalez-sensei from Spain; Fabrizio Mandia-sensei from Italy. Itoh Tomoharu-sensei went to Argentina several times, but not to Buenos Aires' Reshinkan Dojo instead. In the mid 80s, I went to Argentina and visited Cordoba where I became acquainted with Gustavo Adolfo Ramos-sensei. We bonded immediately and have been friends for over 30 years now. Gustavo is not only a great guy, but also has an incredible heart that matches his remarkable Butokuden Dojo in Cordoba.

The Butokuden Dojo has a single characteristic, albeit a very valuable one. It is the deep family feeling among all the members. The dojo really does feel and act like a large family in every sense of the word. Somehow Gustavo has single-handedly been able to create that core feeling since 1985.

Sumi Masatake-sensei's Visit to Cordoba

I have to say that Sumi-sensei is in incredible shape. He travelled from Fukuoka to Toronto, which is about 12 hours, and then flew with me from there to Cordoba, which is about another 10, without a problem. Yamada-sensei also joined us.

Together with Gustavo we organized a schedule that included a combination of the local cuisine, and kendo theory and practice. Oscar Cirone-sensei, founder of Renshinkan Dojo in 1981, from Buenos Aires joined us as well with some folks from his dojo.

Everybody was delighted with the visit and learned an immense amount of new knowledge. Sumi-sensei's style of teaching is impeccable. He is able to make difficult concepts easy to understand. He covered several topics, and the participants had many opportunities to ask him questions on various subjects.

The topics covered were:
- Controlling body movement
- Creating opportunities by approaching and inviting
- Understanding distance
- Optimal striking distances
- *Hasuji*, correct cutting angle
- Correct part of the armour to cut
- Strength and sharpness
- *Yuko-datotsu*
- Projecting your *ki*
- Pressuring the opponent, and what it is to be pressured
- Understanding the concept of *shu- ha-ri*
- *Seme*, *zanshin*, and *tame*

All of the conversations were very rich in content, but one of them in particular resonates with me. Sumi-sensei mentioned that he passed 7-dan in his late 30s and could not try for 8-dan for the next 16 years. Therefore, his challenge was on how to maintain his focus on proper kendo for 16 years, without any deviation at all, maintaining a proper mindset, posture, and execution of techniques. Apparently keeping on the straight and narrow was no easy task, but when the time came to challenge for 8-dan, he passed on his first attempt.

As we exchanged ideas on how to teach and how to correct different points, Yamada-sensei brought to our attention a very important concept: "You can show the camel were the oasis is located; you can show the camel where the water is; but you can't make the camel drink." In other words, you can show proper kendo to a practitioner, but it is up to them to do it correctly and make amendments as they go.

As well as eating delicious *asado*, we also went to Mendoza wine country, and visited the Bodegas Catena Zapata and Kaiken wineries. A truly marvellous event that I recommend to everybody. Time passed very quickly. I would like to express on behalf of Sumi-sensei, Yamada-sensei and myself, a big "thank you" to Kendo Cordoba for being such tremendous hosts, especially to my brother Gustavo Adolfo Ramos for the perfect organisation. Kendo Cordoba always has an open door policy to anybody visiting Argentina who wishes to do *keiko*.

REVIEW:
The Benefits of Lunge Training on Striking Ability

By Michael Ishimatsu-Prime

I recently came across a study that investigated the effect of lunge training on the striking ability of kendo players. Titled "Effects of lunge training on the striking ability of kendo players", it was authored by Tsubaki Takeshi (Kobe Shinawa Women's University), and Maesaka Shigeki, Shimokawa Mika, and Maeda Akira (National Institute of Fitness and Sports in Kanoya).

The researchers employed collegiate kendo athletes to perform lunge training exercises three times a week for four weeks. After this training period, they found that the pull-speed of the left leg during striking (*hikitsuke*), the lunging distance of the right foot, maximal ground reaction force, maximal leg extension power, and the greatest leg split distance all increased significantly even over this short period of time. Their study demonstrated that lunge training was effective in increasing the striking ability (i.e. increasing the pull-speed of the left leg after a strike) of kendo players.

What is considered excellent striking posture is largely contingent on the use of the legs. The authors pointed out that when a strike is made in kendo, a distinction is made between the "stepping foot" (left) and the "stamping foot" (right). The instant a strike is executed, power from the stepping foot is transferred down and back while the body is propelled forward. The left foot is then snapped up behind the right to rectify posture. The ability to do this effectively and powerfully is a decisive factor in kendo matches. For example, the authors quoted other research that demonstrated that winners of the All Japan Kendo Championships had "high plantar flexion strength in the joints of the left foot." In other words, the "ground reaction force of the stamping foot, leg extension power, and plantar flexion strength are necessary to demonstrate a high level of kendo performance." So, how can this be achieved?

Some researchers have focussed on the effectiveness of jump training to increase plantar flexion strength of the stepping foot, *hikitsuke* speed, and improved posture after the strike has been completed. In fact, there are many basic exercises in kendo that seek to improve lower body strength and flexibility. *Matawari-suburi* (lunge swings) in which the left and right feet are alternately slid forward while swinging the *shinai* is useful for improving stability and generating power in the legs.

It was *matawari-suburi* (hereafter "lunge training") that the authors focussed on in their research. They used a 15m rope to mark the target distance that the subjects aimed to reach with their foot. Their normal *fumikomi* distance from *chūdan-no-kamae* was increased by 10% and marked with tape on the rope. Apparently, the average lunging distance for kendo practitioners is 90cm to 130cm, and when a strike is executed at a distance of 20cm longer than one's average, it tends to weaken the strike and stamp.

The authors found that by pushing limits little by little with his kind of lunge training, the subjects were gradually able to improve hip joint extension and flexion in muscle strength around the femur and develop better "hip joint flexibility and the maximal value of ground reaction force". Leg extension power also improved due to an increase in the power of the hamstring and quadriceps muscles. This contributed to better pull-speed of the left foot. The authors did note that they did not observe significant enhancement in hip stability but speculated that this would come with more time.

In any case, it seems that lunge training gave a significant boost to the pouncing distance of the right foot, maximal ground reaction force, maximal leg extension power, leg split distance, and pull speed of the left leg. It's a simple exercise, and is arguably one of the most effective forms of *suburi*.

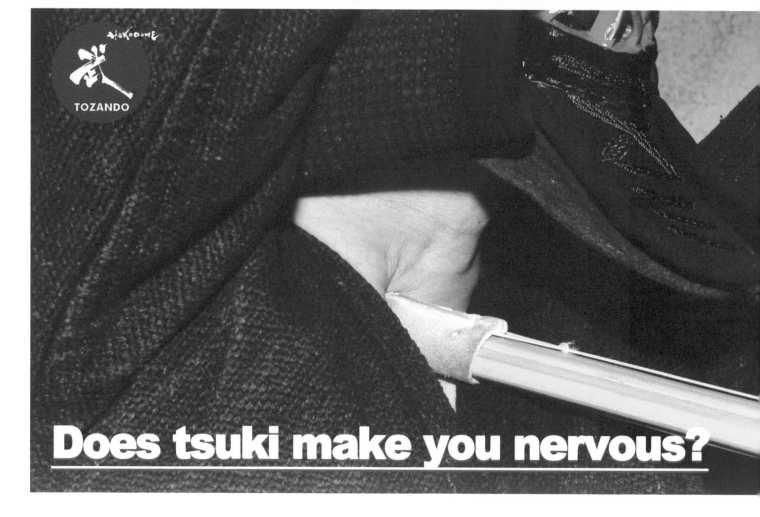

Does tsuki make you nervous?

Tsuki is sometimes regarded as an "advanced" technique, something you need skill and experience to pull off effectively and safely. This is sometimes extrapolated into "you shouldn't practice tsuki yet because it is dangerous" or "you don't have enough experience yet to learn tsuki".

In reality, tsuki is a core part of your Kendo experience. If you aren't learning tsuki, then that is one of four fundamental techniques you are not experiencing. However, if your partners practice tsuki haphazardly or you only encounter desperate attempts in shiai then naturally you will want to avoid tsuki.

Tozando developed the Ideal Safety Guard (ISG) not only to provide protection, but also to allow you to receive tsuki with confidence. When you use the ISG, tsuki can become like any other technique. You can rely on it to protect you when you need it, so you can focus with getting on with training.

Tsuki should be a positive experience for both kakarite and motodachi. We want to remove the stigma surrounding tsuki, so that kendoka around the world can develop strong, positive and safe kendo. This is why we decided to develop the ISG.

The best part about the ISG is that it is always there and will fall into place even if your head is tilted back. This helps people inexperienced with tsuki feel confident that they have every protection available. If you are more confident receiving tsuki you will become more confident delivering it as well and then your technique will also improve.

With the ISG you don't need to be afraid of tsuki. It allows you to throw yourself into training and not only get used to tsuki, but develop it as you would men or kote or do.

ve you ever
eceived a dangerous tsuki?

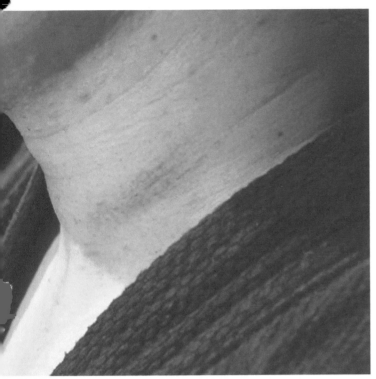

When a tsuki goes wrong it can be very dangerous. Most of us can handle bruises and knocks, but a shinai getting caught under your men can do a lot of damage. Whilst rare, it's worth not taking the chance.

Delivering and receiving tsuki requires discipline. When you perform tsuki you need to create an opening and opportunity with pressure just like any other technique. Firing off random, or poorly timed tsuki will likely miss and can be very dangerous.

Tozando's ISG helps foster a calm and relaxed mindset not only when practicing tsuki in kihon, but in the more pressured environments of jigeiko and shiai.

If your opponent lacks discipline the ISG will be there to protect your neck.

Can accidents still happen?

Even if you are exercising discipline and understand tsuki well, there are times when accidents are unavoidable. The kensen of the shinai slipping off your do's mune and up towards your neck is a good example.

The Ideal Safety Guard's patented design means that whether your chin is up or down the guard hangs close to your neck.
Even if the kensen slips under your ago from below the ISG will be there to prevent serious injury.

Available across a wide range of bogu the ISG is useful to any level of kendoka. Bring confidence and peace of mind to your training with our Ideal Safety Guard—tsuki is no longer something that needs to be avoided, with the ISG practice and receive tsuki fearlessly!

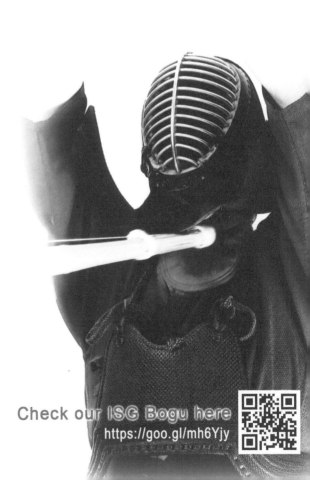

Check our ISG Bogu here
https://goo.gl/mh6Yjy